The ChatGPT Playbook: Mastering Prompts for Exceptional UX Design

By

Lorraine Phillips

360 Books, LLC

Atlanta, GA

Author: Lorraine Phillips
Cover and interior design: Lorraine Phillips

Website: uxwithchatgpt.com

ISBN-13: 979-8-9885658-0-2
LCCN: 2023941513

Library of Congress subject headings:
1. Artificial intelligence.
2. User interfaces (Computer systems).

Published by:
360 Books, LLC
PO Box 361721
Atlanta, GA 30036

First Printing
Printed in the United States of America

Table of Contents

Introduction

Well, you have Gary Vaynerchuk to blame for this one. While watching one of his instructional videos on YouTube, I heard him say something along the lines of "It takes a minimum of 50 hours before you can consider yourself somewhat of an expert in something." And that was it. I immediately downloaded a timer from the App Store and got to work, consuming everything I could get my hands on with regards to ChatGPT and prompt engineering. I remember completing four courses in that very first week. The challenge was on!

Now, I know the term "expert" has been loosely thrown around since the inception of social media, but in my humble opinion, the days of studying something for four to six years before considering oneself an expert are long gone–at least within the field of IT. And there's nothing (and I mean nothing) that can beat the practical application of knowledge you gain.

I delved so deep that I eventually forgot to start and stop the timer every time I got ready to absorb information. However, I do know that I surpassed that number a long time ago. And along with learning about ChatGPT and prompt engineering, I decided to use the tool to help me author my new book, the one you have in your hands right now, as a way for me to practice these newly acquired skills.

It's been a super weird but extremely rewarding experience. There were areas in my brain that I no longer needed to use as a writer, but instead had to replace them with skills that would allow me to manipulate the tool to get it to do what I wanted, in exactly the way I wanted as well.

There were definitely good and bad days. Sometimes ChatGPT would work like a dream, and at other times would frustrate me to no end. But that's been *my* experience. The one thing I'm absolutely certain of is that ChatGPT cannot replace me. And when you think about it, really, how could it? After all, I had to teach it how to be me (I provided it with samples of my writing and asked the model to emulate my style and tone for various sections of the book)–and even then I'd have to keep constantly fine-tuning. And, as good as it is, I can tell when text has been generated by the model because it's often dull, boring, and dry. It's not until you learn how to direct and manipulate the output to the way that you want, will you get satisfactory results.

So, after 50+ hours and a book on the subject, do I consider myself a prompt expert? Hmm, I'd like to say that I'm still on the path of continuous learning. But I *did* get ChatGPT to help me generate over 300 useful UX prompts in a matter of weeks, which has absolutely blown my mind. It was a concept I dreamt up and a challenge I set for myself, so to be able to manipulate the tool to accomplish just that is nothing short of amazing to me.

As a result, I'd simply put it like this: if there's a train that's getting ready to leave, then I'd say that I'm at least at the station, and the reason why I'd put it that way is because none of us have any idea of what's coming next. But the fact that you're reading this lets me know that you're just as curious and ready as I am. So, on that note, let's begin.

Chapter 1: What is AI?

Artificial Intelligence (AI) has emerged as a transformative technology, simulating human intelligence in machines to perform tasks that typically require human cognitive abilities. The field of AI encompasses various techniques and algorithms, each serving different purposes and employing distinct methodologies. Here are few examples of the different types of AI, their applications, and the challenges and considerations associated with AI development and deployment.

1. **Rule-based systems:**
   Rule-based systems operate by following a set of predefined rules to make decisions. These rules are typically formulated by human experts who encode their knowledge into the system. Rule-based AI is often used in applications where the problem domain is well-defined and can be explicitly represented in the form of rules. For example, expert systems in healthcare can diagnose diseases based on a set of medical guidelines. These systems rely on the expertise of human specialists to create a knowledge base of rules that the AI system can utilize for decision-making.

2. **Machine learning:**
   Machine learning involves algorithms that learn from data and improve their performance through experience. It can be broadly categorized into two types: supervised learning and unsupervised learning.

   In supervised learning, the algorithm is provided with labeled examples from which it learns to make predictions or decisions. For instance, spam email filters are trained on labeled examples of spam and non-spam emails to classify incoming messages. The algorithm learns to recognize patterns and features in the data that distinguish spam from legitimate emails.

   Unsupervised learning, on the other hand, involves finding patterns or structures in unlabeled data. Clustering algorithms, for instance, group similar data points together without prior knowledge of their labels. This type of machine learning is useful in tasks such as customer segmentation, anomaly detection, and data exploration.

3. **Deep learning:**
   Deep learning is a subset of machine learning that has gained significant attention in recent years. It revolves around artificial neural networks (ANNs), which are inspired by the structure and functioning of the human brain. Deep learning algorithms consist of multiple layers of interconnected nodes, or neurons, which process and transform data.

   Each layer learns increasingly complex features from the input data, leading to hierarchical representations. Deep learning has proven to be particularly effective in domains where the input data has a high dimensionality, such as image and speech recognition. Applications like facial recognition in photos and voice assistants like Siri and Alexa rely on deep learning techniques.

The success of deep learning is largely attributed to advancements in computational power, the availability of large datasets, and the development of specialized hardware, such as graphics processing units (GPUs), which can accelerate the training and inference processes.

4. **Reinforcement learning:**
   Reinforcement learning is a type of machine learning where algorithms learn to make decisions through trial and error. The algorithms interact with an environment and receive feedback in the form of rewards or penalties based on their actions.

   By exploring the environment and learning from the consequences of their actions, reinforcement learning algorithms can develop strategies to maximize the cumulative rewards over time. This approach has been successful in domains such as game playing, robotics, and autonomous systems.

   Onc notable example of reinforcement learning is AlphaGo, an AI program developed by DeepMind. AlphaGo defeated the world champion Go player using a combination of deep neural networks and reinforcement learning techniques. This achievement showcased the potential of reinforcement learning in complex decision-making tasks.

5. **Natural Language Processing (NLP):**
   Natural language processing focuses on enabling computers to understand, interpret, and generate human language. It encompasses tasks such as speech recognition, language translation, sentiment analysis, and question-answering systems.

   NLP techniques enable virtual personal assistants like Siri and Alexa to interpret voice commands and provide responses or perform tasks. These systems employ various AI components, including speech recognition, natural language understanding, and dialogue management, to interact with users in a conversational manner.

Recent advancements in NLP, particularly with the use of deep learning models such as transformers, have significantly improved the accuracy and fluency of language generation and understanding tasks. This has led to applications such as chatbots, language translation services, and voice-controlled smart home devices.

6. **Computer Vision:**
   Computer vision enables machines to understand and interpret visual information from images or videos. It involves tasks like object detection, image recognition, facial recognition, and image segmentation.

   Computer vision algorithms analyze pixel data to extract meaningful features and recognize objects or patterns in images. These algorithms are trained on large annotated datasets to learn to identify specific objects or attributes in new images.

   Applications of computer vision are numerous and diverse. They range from autonomous vehicles that use computer vision to detect and track objects on the road, to surveillance systems that can recognize individuals or detect suspicious activities in crowded areas. Computer vision is also used in augmented reality applications, medical image analysis, quality control in manufacturing, and many other fields.

7. **Knowledge Representation and Reasoning:**
   Knowledge representation and reasoning focus on representing knowledge in a structured form that machines can process. It involves techniques for organizing and storing knowledge, as well as reasoning mechanisms for making inferences and drawing conclusions.

Various formalisms and languages have been developed for knowledge representation, including ontologies, semantic networks, and logic-based languages. These representations enable AI systems to capture and manipulate domain-specific knowledge and reason about complex relationships and dependencies.

Knowledge representation and reasoning have applications in fields such as expert systems, intelligent tutoring systems, and decision support systems. These systems rely on a rich knowledge base and reasoning mechanisms to provide expert-level advice or guidance in specific domains.

8. **Cognitive Computing:**
   Cognitive computing combines various AI techniques to simulate human thought processes, including perception, reasoning, learning, and problem-solving. It aims to create AI systems that can understand and interact with humans in a more natural and intelligent manner.

   Cognitive computing systems often incorporate elements of machine learning, natural language processing, computer vision, and knowledge representation and reasoning. These systems can process vast amounts of data, learn from experience, and adapt to changing circumstances.

   The goal of cognitive computing is to enable AI systems to not only perform specific tasks but also understand context, reason about complex situations, and engage in meaningful conversations. This has applications in areas such as healthcare diagnostics, customer service, intelligent assistants, and personalized recommendations.

9. **Generative Models:**
   Generative AI is another important type of AI that focuses on creating new content based on learned patterns. Generative models,

such as Generative Adversarial Networks (GANs) and Variational Autoencoders (VAEs), are used to generate new data that resembles the training data they were exposed to.

Generative AI has diverse applications across various domains. For example, in the field of computer vision, generative models can be used to synthesize realistic images or transform images in creative ways. In natural language processing, generative models can generate coherent and contextually relevant text, which has applications in chatbots, language generation, and content creation. Another exciting application of generative AI is in the realm of art and design. Artists and designers can leverage generative models to create unique and novel visual or auditory experiences.

ChatGPT, short for Generative Pre-trained Transformer, is an example of a generative AI model specifically designed for facilitating natural language conversations. It utilizes deep learning techniques, particularly transformer-based neural networks, to understand and generate human-like text responses. Using this ability, ChatGPT has found applications in customer support chatbots, virtual assistants, content generation, and creative writing. By leveraging generative AI capabilities, ChatGPT aims to simulate human-like conversation and provide users with valuable information and assistance.

AI algorithms heavily rely on the availability of data for training models, allowing them to learn patterns, generalize from examples, and make accurate predictions. The more diverse and representative the data, the better the AI system's ability to handle a wide range of inputs. However, it is essential to ensure that the data used for training is unbiased and does not perpetuate discriminatory or harmful biases.

AI has become ubiquitous in our daily lives, impacting various aspects of society. Virtual personal assistants, such as Siri and Alexa, leverage AI technologies to understand voice commands and perform tasks like setting reminders, providing weather updates, or playing music. These assistants utilize natural language processing techniques to interpret and respond to human speech.

AI is also revolutionizing industries and domains beyond consumer applications. In healthcare, AI is employed for medical image analysis, disease diagnosis, personalized treatment recommendation, and drug discovery. AI algorithms can process and interpret medical images like X-rays, MRIs, and CT scans, aiding radiologists in detecting anomalies and assisting in diagnosis. Additionally, AI can analyze patient data and medical records to identify patterns and predict the likelihood of certain diseases.

In finance, AI algorithms are utilized for fraud detection, algorithmic trading, credit scoring, and risk assessment. These algorithms can analyze vast amounts of financial data, identify suspicious patterns, and make real-time decisions to mitigate risks. They can also assess creditworthiness by analyzing an individual's financial history and other relevant factors.

AI is also making significant contributions to the field of education. AI-powered adaptive learning systems can tailor educational content and instructional approaches based on individual student needs and preferences. These systems analyze student performance data, identify areas of weakness, and provide personalized feedback and guidance. AI-powered tutoring systems can support students by offering additional explanations, practice exercises, and real-time assistance, helping them overcome challenges and improve their performance.

While AI offers numerous benefits and opportunities, it also raises important considerations and challenges. Ethical concerns related to privacy, bias, transparency, and accountability are crucial in AI development and deployment. Ensuring that AI systems are fair, transparent, and accountable requires ongoing research, regulation, and responsible practices.

Privacy concerns arise due to the vast amounts of personal data collected and processed by AI systems. Safeguarding this data and ensuring its responsible use is essential to protect individuals' privacy rights. Measures such as modifying or removing identifying information from datasets, ensuring secure data storage, and obtaining consent from individuals are crucial in preserving privacy.

Bias in AI algorithms is another significant concern. AI systems learn from historical data, which may contain biases reflecting societal prejudices and inequalities. These biases can be perpetuated and amplified by AI systems, leading to discriminatory outcomes. Addressing bias requires careful attention to the data used for training, the evaluation of algorithmic fairness, and the development of mitigation strategies.

Transparency and interpretability of AI systems are essential for building trust and understanding. Complex AI models, such as deep neural networks, can be highly opaque, making it challenging to explain their decision-making processes. Research efforts are focused on developing techniques for explaining and interpreting AI models to ensure they can be audited, validated, and understood.

Accountability in AI systems is critical to ensure responsible use and mitigate potential risks. Establishing clear lines of responsibility and accountability, as well as mechanisms for monitoring and auditing AI systems, is crucial to address any unintended consequences or harmful outcomes.

As AI continues to evolve and advance, ongoing research, collaboration, and a multidisciplinary approach will be essential in harnessing its full potential while mitigating risks and ensuring its beneficial impact on society.

Chapter 2:
About ChatGPT

ChatGPT is an advanced chatbot developed by OpenAI and introduced to the public in November 2022. It represents a significant breakthrough in natural language processing and builds upon the success of OpenAI's GPT-3.5 models. We'll explore the concept of large language models, the training process of ChatGPT, how it understands natural language, and the implications of its language generation capabilities.

Understanding Large Language Models

A large language model is a sophisticated computer program designed to comprehend and generate human language. It leverages deep learning techniques and neural networks to analyze vast amounts of text data and learn the patterns and rules of language. By understanding the relationships between words and sentences, these models can predict the most appropriate words to follow in a given context. They acquire a deep knowledge of language that enables them to perform various language-related tasks with remarkable accuracy and fluency.

Training Data

To achieve its impressive language capabilities, GPT-3 (the predecessor to ChatGPT) underwent extensive training on a dataset comprising 45 terabytes of text data sourced from the internet. The data encompassed a wide range of sources, including web pages, articles, books, blogs, social media posts, online forums, news sources, research papers, scientific journals, and more. The extensive collection of text encompassed a wide range of topics and fields, including science and technology, medicine and healthcare, business and finance, politics and government, art and culture, sports and entertainment, as well as education and academia.

The training process involved a method known as "unsupervised learning," where the model learned from the data without specific human guidance. It analyzed the text data, identified patterns, and built a language model that captures the statistical regularities of human language.

ChatGPT's Fine-Tuning and Supervised Learning

Once the initial training was completed, the model underwent a process called fine-tuning. During fine-tuning, the model was exposed to additional data that had been specially curated and reviewed by human experts. This curated dataset helped refine the model's understanding of specific domains, improved its response quality, and reduced biases. The fine-tuning process employed a method called "supervised fine-tuning," where a human instructor guided and taught the model how to perform various language-related tasks effectively.

Understanding Natural Language

Natural language refers to the way humans communicate and express themselves through words. While the English language consists of over 170,000 words, most English-speaking adults possess a vocabulary of approximately 42,000 words. However, only about 25% of these words are frequently used in everyday life. ChatGPT leverages this knowledge to generate sensible, logical responses that are fitting to the conversation.

By training on vast amounts of text data, ChatGPT has learned the patterns and rules of natural language. It utilizes this knowledge to calculate the probability of the next word in a sentence based on the likelihood of specific words being used in conjunction with one another. This probabilistic approach allows ChatGPT to generate coherent and contextually appropriate responses, aligning with the patterns observed in human language.

Implications of ChatGPT's Language Understanding

The language understanding and generation capabilities of ChatGPT have significant implications in various domains. Businesses can utilize it to enhance customer support by providing quick and accurate responses to inquiries. It can assist in language translation, making it easier for individuals to communicate across different languages and cultures. Educators can utilize ChatGPT to offer personalized learning experiences and assist students with their assignments. Additionally, ChatGPT has potential applications in content generation, creative writing, and even entertainment.

To Sum It All Up

ChatGPT represents a remarkable advancement in natural language processing. Through its training on vast amounts of text data and its understanding of natural language, ChatGPT has acquired an extensive knowledge of language patterns and rules. This enables it to produce logical and contextually fitting replies in a conversational style. Its language understanding capabilities have significant implications in various domains, including customer support, translation, education, and content generation. As OpenAI continues to refine its models, ChatGPT paves the way for more sophisticated and human-like conversational AI systems, transforming human interaction with automated language technologies.

ChatGPT Uses

Although truly infinite in nature, uses for ChatGPT can include:

- **Summarizing articles:** ChatGPT can condense lengthy articles into concise summaries.
- **Generating presentation outlines:** ChatGPT can assist in creating structured outlines for presentations.
- **Writing business letters:** ChatGPT can compose professional letters for various business purposes.
- **Writing emails and messages:** ChatGPT can help draft effective emails and messages.
- **Writing documentation:** ChatGPT can generate documentation for different purposes.
- **Improving resumes:** ChatGPT can offer suggestions and tips to enhance resumes.
- **Preparing for interviews:** ChatGPT can simulate job interview scenarios and provide practice questions.
- **Crafting profiles:** ChatGPT can help create engaging profiles for individuals or businesses.
- **Composing songs:** ChatGPT can assist in songwriting and creating lyrics.
- **Crafting book and blog titles:** ChatGPT can generate compelling titles for books and blog posts.
- **Creating social media captions:** ChatGPT can generate catchy captions for social media posts.
- **Authoring a book:** ChatGPT can help with the writing process of a book. (I can definitely attest to this one.)

- **Developing a children's TV show storyline:** ChatGPT can assist in developing engaging storylines for children's TV shows.
- **Creating scripts:** ChatGPT can generate scripts for video or film.
- **Brainstorming product ideas:** ChatGPT can help generate innovative ideas for new products.
- **Developing a business plan:** ChatGPT can assist in creating comprehensive business plans.
- **Carrying out competitive analysis:** ChatGPT can analyze market trends, identify competitors' strategies, and offer insights into their strengths and weaknesses.
- **Defining a brand voice:** ChatGPT can assist in establishing a consistent brand voice and tone.
- **Identifying key features or benefits of a product:** ChatGPT can highlight the main features and benefits of a product.
- **Assisting with product launches:** ChatGPT can offer support in planning and executing product launches.
- **Researching target audiences for products:** ChatGPT can gather information about potential target audiences for products.
- **Identifying niches:** ChatGPT can help identify specific target markets or niches.
- **Seeking marketing help and advice:** ChatGPT can provide guidance and suggestions for marketing strategies.
- **Providing research assistance:** ChatGPT can aid in conducting research on various topics.
- **Finding resources:** ChatGPT can assist in locating relevant resources for specific topics or projects.
- **Analyzing data:** ChatGPT can leverage its capabilities to process and analyze data, providing valuable insights and assisting in data analysis tasks.
- **Assisting with studying and learning information:** ChatGPT can generate quizzes, vocabulary lists, and provide interactive learning experiences.

- **Assisting in language learning:** ChatGPT can generate language exercises, vocabulary lists, and hold simple conversations to aid in language learning.
- **Providing legal help and documentation:** ChatGPT can offer general assistance and generate basic legal documents.
- **Planning trips with a specified budget:** ChatGPT can offer information, suggest destinations, and help in planning trips within a specified budget.
- **Assisting with event scheduling:** ChatGPT can help organize and schedule events like conferences.
- **Creating checklists:** ChatGPT generates comprehensive checklists for project management, event planning, or task organization. It provides step-by-step instructions, prioritizes tasks, and offers suggestions for efficient and organized completion.
- **Providing technical support:** ChatGPT can offer guidance and troubleshooting assistance for technical issues.
- **Being a coding assistant:** ChatGPT can assist with coding tasks by offering guidance, suggestions, and helping you debug code.
- **Helping with SEO:** ChatGPT can suggest strategies and techniques to improve search engine optimization.
- **Offering relationship advice:** ChatGPT can provide guidance and suggestions for various relationship issues.
- **Serving as a life coach:** ChatGPT can provide guidance and support in various aspects of life.
- **Improving overall health:** ChatGPT can offer tips and advice for improving overall health and well-being.
- **Creating workout programs:** ChatGPT can generate personalized workout programs based on fitness goals and preferences.
- **Creating meal plans:** ChatGPT can generate personalized meal plans based on dietary preferences and requirements.

As you can see, ChatGPT as your copilot opens up a world of opportunities for productivity, creativity, and problem-solving.

ChatGPT Limitations

It's important for budding prompt engineers to familiarize themselves with the limitations of ChatGPT. Like any AI technology, ChatGPT has weaknesses and challenges. By understanding these limitations, prompt engineers can gain insights into the potential drawbacks and challenges of implementing AI language models, enabling them to set realistic expectations for ChatGPT's capabilities. Here are just a few:

Lacks empathy and emotional intelligence: ChatGPT does not possess genuine emotions or empathy. It responds based on learned patterns without truly understanding or empathizing with the user's emotions or needs. This can lead to technically accurate responses that lack sensitivity and emotional support, which may be necessary in certain situations.

Unable to make human-like judgments: ChatGPT doesn't possess human-like judgment capabilities. It lacks moral reasoning, ethical frameworks, and the ability to weigh conflicting values to make subjective decisions. Its responses are solely based on patterns learned from data, which can sometimes result in morally or ethically questionable outputs.

Unable to reason or think critically: ChatGPT lacks the ability to engage in complex reasoning or critical thinking. While it can provide information based on patterns in the training data, it may struggle to evaluate multiple perspectives, consider long-term consequences, or analyze complex arguments. Users should exercise caution when relying on ChatGPT for decision-making or complex problem-solving.

Has limited understanding of context and nuance: ChatGPT struggles with comprehending context and nuanced queries. Without sufficient context, the model may generate off-topic, misleading, or inaccurate responses.

Is dependent on training data: ChatGPT's performance heavily relies on the quality, diversity, and representativeness of the training data. If the training data is limited or contains inaccuracies, the model may struggle to provide accurate or comprehensive responses.

Is vulnerable to bias and influence: ChatGPT is trained on large datasets that reflect biases present in the data. If the training data contains biased or unbalanced perspectives, the model can inadvertently reproduce or amplify those biases. Biased or leading prompts can influence the model, potentially generating unfair or biased responses.

Has a knowledge cutoff date: ChatGPT is not aware of events or information that occurred after its training data was last updated. This can limit the model's ability to provide accurate, up-to-date responses.

Lacks source citation and fact-checking abilities: ChatGPT does not provide sources or citations for the information it generates. While it can offer general knowledge based on its training data, it lacks the ability to accurately cite sources. Since ChatGPT does not have internet access and does not remember the specific origins of its information, it often generates sources that may appear credible but are actually inaccurate. Therefore, it is crucial to independently verify the information obtained from ChatGPT to ensure accuracy and reliability.

The training data is censored: ChatGPT has been designed to avoid generating certain types of content, such as hate speech, explicit material, or controversial topics. While this censorship promotes responsible usage, it can also result in the model avoiding or providing incomplete responses on certain topics, limiting its usefulness in those areas.

Has memory limitations: ChatGPT has the ability to remember what was discussed earlier in a conversation but only to a certain extent. As of GPT-4, ChatGPT's memory capacity is 32,768 tokens. A single word usually consists of 1 to 3 tokens, meaning that ChatGPT can retain up to around 10,000 words at a time. If your input or output text exceeds this limit, the model may lose or truncate information. If, by chance, a response unexpectedly pauses mid-flow, simply click the "Continue generating" button to resume the process.

Has issues with complex math problems: ChatGPT possesses the ability to perform fundamental mathematical calculations like addition, subtraction, multiplication, and division. However, it is not specifically designed to serve as a complex math problem solver or a dedicated mathematical software so may not deliver advanced mathematical solutions or handle complex mathematical concepts as effectively as dedicated mathematical tools.

Can "hallucinate" and generate fictional content: ChatGPT has been observed to hallucinate, meaning it may generate responses that are fictional or entirely made up. This can happen when the model tries to provide an answer despite lacking the necessary information or encountering ambiguous queries. Once again, users should exercise caution when relying on ChatGPT for information that is not supported by reliable sources.

Chapter 3: Prompt Engineering

What is Prompt Engineering?

Prompt engineering is a meticulous process that involves crafting and fine-tuning prompts for natural language processing (NLP) models like ChatGPT, chatbots, or virtual assistants. The goal is to create prompts that are clear, concise, and capable of generating valuable outcomes. The quality of the prompt directly impacts the quality of the response you receive. Hence, the better the prompt, the better the output.

Iteration plays a vital role in the prompt design process. Each iteration should build upon insights gained from previous results, aiming to address limitations or inaccuracies encountered along the way. For instance, if the initial prompt yields a vague result or the model generates an off-topic response, you should revise the prompt to offer more precise instructions or provide additional context. To generate effective prompts consider the following guidelines:

- **Use plain language:** Avoid jargon, overly complex terms, or ambiguous language in your prompts.

- **Be specific and provide clear details:** Clearly state what you are looking for or the type of information you need.
- **Include context:** Provide relevant background information or context to help the model understand the desired focus or perspective.
- **Arrange prompts logically and coherently:** Structure your prompts in a logical and coherent manner so instructions can easily be followed.
- **Provide constraints (if necessary):** If there are any limitations or constraints to consider, make them clear in the prompt.
- **Provide instructions on style, tone, length, structure, or format:** If you have specific requirements for the output, such as a particular style, tone, length, structure, or format, make sure to include those instructions within your prompt.
- **Ask follow-up questions:** If the model's response is unclear or you need more information, ask follow-up questions to clarify uncertainties and provide the necessary context.
- **Provide examples:** Use examples to illustrate the desired output, whether it's related to style, tone, structure, or format. Examples help the model understand your expectations more clearly.
- **Experiment with different approaches:** Explore different prompt variations and perspectives to find the most effective way to elicit the desired response from the model.

By following these guidelines and continuously refining your prompts through iteration, you can enhance the performance and accuracy of NLP models like ChatGPT to generate more valuable and relevant responses.

A Formula for Success

The age-old saying "garbage in, garbage out" remains just as relevant today as it always has. I've put together a formula that contains the essential building blocks for creating effective prompts. A well-crafted prompt can include any (or all) of the following criteria, which should be customized or tailored to meet the specific requirement of the task or question at hand.

Formula: [Role] [Task or Question] [Context] [Goal] [Constraints] [Style or Tone][Structure or Format]

Now, let's break that down.

[Role]: This represents the specific role or entity for whom the prompt is being created. It could be a job title, a group of people, or any other relevant identifier. ChatGPT can act as any role or expert you'd like from a career counselor to a personal trainer to a lawyer to a real estate agent to a travel guide to a hypnotherapist to a life coach to an investment manager–you name it, ChatGPT can assume it. Specifying the role helps tailor the prompt to the specific needs or perspective of that role.

[Task or Question]: This element defines the specific task or question the prompt aims to address. It should be clear and concise, describing the objective or the problem to be solved. The task or question should be formulated in a way that guides the prompt towards generating a relevant response.

[Context]: This element provides additional information or background that is necessary to understand the task or question fully. Think along the lines of who (target audience), what, where, when, why, or how. Including relevant context helps the prompt generator better understand the scenario and generate a more contextually appropriate response.

[Goal]: This element outlines the desired outcome or objective of the task or question. It clarifies what the role is trying to achieve or accomplish. Defining the goal helps the prompt generator focus on providing information or guidance that is directly relevant to achieving that goal.

[Constraints]: Constraints define any limitations, restrictions, or conditions that need to be taken into consideration while completing the task. They provide context about what must be adhered to or considered during the process. For instance, you can instruct ChatGPT to keep the response within 200 words, meaning it should not exceed that limit. By specifying constraints, you help direct the prompt generator by setting boundaries or limitations that are necessary for the task.

[Style or Tone]: This element specifies the desired style or tone of the generated output. It can include considerations for the writing style such as formal, informal, technical, professional, conversational, etc. Additionally, it encompasses the tone of the response, such as friendly, authoritative, persuasive, etc. Providing clear instructions about the desired style or tone aids in guiding the generated output.

[Structure or Format]: This element defines the preferred structure or format. It includes instructions regarding the organization of the response, such as the use of bullet points, paragraphs, headings, or any other type of structural element. Additionally, it encompasses the desired format of the response, such as plain text, code snippets, examples, tables, or any other specific format requirements. Specifying the desired structure or format ensures that the generated output is presented in a manner that is suitable for your needs.

By utilizing this formula and customizing each element you can create effective prompts that yield desired results. Always remember, the quality of the prompt will directly influence the quality of the response you receive.

The Formula in Action

Here's an example of the formula in action. In chapter 6 we'll explore many more that have been specifically created for UX practitioners.

[Role]: Marketing specialist
[Task or Question]: Create 3 emails all ending with a call to action.
[Context]: The emails are for my online audience of TikTok creators.
[Goal]: The goal is to drive sales to my product.
[Constraints]: Less than 250 words
[Style or Tone]: Friendly and engaging
[Structure or Format]: Email style

Prompt: You are a marketing specialist. Create 3 emails ending with a call to action. The goal is to drive sales to my product. The emails are for my audience of TikTok creators, they should be friendly and engaging and less than 250 words.

Run the prompt as-is and you'll be pretty amazed by the results. To tailor the response to your specific need, start (or prime) the chat with prompts like these.

Prompt: I am going to give you a description of my product. Do you understand?

ChatGPT: Yes, I understand. Please go ahead and provide a description of your product, and I'll do my best to assist you.

Prompt: [Provide your product description]

ChatGPT will then provide a summary of the info you just typed in.

Prompt: Now I'm going to give you a description of my target audience. Do you understand?

ChatGPT: Yes, I understand. Please provide a description of your target audience, and I'll do my best to assist you.

Prompt: [Provide a description of your target audience]

ChatGPT will then provide a summary of the info you just typed in.

Now run the original prompt again and see the difference in the output the model provides. In the upcoming chapter, we'll explore some of the elements found within the prompt formula and provide ideas for their practical application.

Chapter 4: Insights for Effective Formula Application

Role Prompting / Act As

Here are a few examples of the "act as" prompt, along with ideas on what that particular role can do or be used for. These straightforward prompts can actually be entered directly into ChatGPT. As you proceed through the chapter, you'll discover additional criteria you can apply to further refine your prompts in order to generate more precise, customized outcomes–the ultimate goal of prompt engineering.

Act as an **Advertiser**
Design a catchy slogan for a new energy drink

Act as a **Composer**
Compose a short melody for a romantic scene in a film

Act as a **Debate Moderator**
Facilitate a debate on the topic of climate change

Act as a **Doctor providing creative treatments**
Recommend alternative therapies for managing chronic pain

Act as an **Environmental Consultant**
Propose sustainable practices for a manufacturing company to reduce their carbon footprint

Act as an **Event Planner**
Organize a virtual conference on entrepreneurship for minority women

Act as a **Financial Advisor**
Create a personalized investment plan for a client with a moderate risk appetite

Act as a **Friend**
Offer advice to a friend who is going through a tough breakup

Act as a **Game Developer**
Design a level for a puzzle game with increasing difficulty

Act as a **Health and Fitness Coach**
Create a workout routine for someone looking to improve their cardiovascular fitness

Act as a **Historical Figure**
Describe your experiences during a significant event in history

Act as a **Hypnotherapist**
Guide a client through a relaxation and visualization session to help reduce anxiety

Act as an **Instructor teaching algorithms**
Explain the concept of recursion using a simple example

Act as an **Interviewer**
Conduct an interview with a job candidate for a software engineering position

Act as a **Legal Advisor**
Provide legal advice on copyright infringement in the digital age

Act as a **Life Coach 1**
Help someone set goals and create an action plan for personal growth

Act as a **Life Coach 2**
Summarize [book title] self-help book and highlight its key principles

Act as a **Magician**
Perform a card trick that leaves the audience amazed

Act as a **Marketing Strategist**
Develop a marketing campaign for a new smartphone targeting young professionals

Act as a **Mental Health Adviser**
Offer coping strategies for managing anxiety in daily life

Act as a **Movie Critic**
Write a review of the latest superhero movie and provide a rating out of 5 stars

Act as a **Motivational Coach**
Deliver an inspiring speech to motivate individuals to pursue their dreams

Act as a **Motivational Speaker**
Share a personal success story and offer advice on overcoming obstacles

Act as a **Music Critic**
Critique a recent album release from a popular artist

Act as a **Novelist**
Write the opening paragraph of a suspenseful thriller novel

Act as a **Personal Chef**
Create a gourmet menu for a dinner party with dietary restrictions

Act as a **Personal Stylist**
Suggest a trendy outfit for a special occasion based on the client's preferences

Act as a **Personal Trainer**
Demonstrate proper form and technique for a basic strength training exercise

Act as a **Philosopher**
Reflect on the meaning of life and the pursuit of happiness

Act as a **Plagiarism Checker**
Analyze a given text and determine if it contains any instances of plagiarism

Act as a **Poet**
Compose a short poem about the beauty of nature

Act as a **Product Recommendation Expert**
Recommend the best smartphone for a tech-savvy consumer

Act as a **Proofreader**
Proofread for spelling, grammar, and readability. Then give me a list of changes you made.

Act as a **Public Speaking Coach**
Provide tips for overcoming stage fright and delivering a confident speech

Act as a **Rapper**
Write a verse for a rap song about resilience and perseverance

Act as a **Relationship Coach**
Advise a couple on improving communication and resolving conflicts

Act as a **Screenwriter**
Outline the plot and main characters for a romantic comedy film

Act as a **Self-Help Book**
Write a chapter on building self-esteem and developing a positive mindset

Act as a **Social Media Influencer**
Create an engaging Instagram post promoting a new skincare product

Act as a **Song Recommende**r
Suggest a playlist of uplifting songs for a road trip

Act as a **Stand-up Comedian**
Tell a funny anecdote about a recent embarrassing moment

Act as a **Storyteller**
Narrate a short fable with a moral lesson

Act as a **Tech Reviewer**
Evaluate the latest smartwatch, highlighting its features and drawbacks

Act as a **Technical Support**
Troubleshoot a computer issue remotely and guide the user through the solution

Act as a **Text-based Excel**
Calculate the sum of a column of numbers in a text-based Excel sheet

Act as a **Text Summarizer**
Summarize this for me, highlighting key takeaways and themes: [insert text from source]

Act as a **Travel Guide**
Recommend the top attractions to visit in a city known for its historical landmarks

Act as a **UX/UI Developer**
Design a user-friendly interface for a mobile banking app

Act as a **Virtual Assistant**
Schedule a meeting and set reminders for important tasks

Act as a **Web Design Consultant**
Advise a client on optimizing their website's navigation and user experience

Task Verbs

Here is a list of 85 verbs that can be used as a part of your task instruction or question. Refer to the previous "Role Prompting / Act As" section to see how some of these verbs can be practically applied.

- Adapt
- Advise
- Analyze
- Annotate

- Argue
- Assess
- Brainstorm
- Calculate
- Change
- Classify
- Collaborate
- Compare
- Compose
- Conclude
- Condense
- Conduct
- Construct
- Contribute
- Craft
- Create
- Critique
- Defend
- Define
- Deliver
- Demonstrate
- Describe
- Design
- Develop
- Draft
- Edit
- Elaborate
- Enhance
- Evaluate
- Examine
- Explain
- Facilitate

- Formulate
- Generate
- Guide
- Help
- Highlight
- Identify
- Implement
- Incorporate
- Interpret
- Investigate
- List
- Manage
- Modify
- Narrate
- Navigate
- Offer
- Optimize
- Order
- Organize
- Outline
- Paraphrase
- Perform
- Persuade
- Present
- Proofread
- Propose
- Provide
- Recommend
- Refine
- Reflect
- Research

- Revise
- Reword
- Rewrite
- Schedule
- Share
- Suggest
- Sum up
- Summarize
- Support
- Synthesize
- Tell
- Train
- Transform
- Translate
- Troubleshoot
- Utilize
- Validate
- Write

Output Parameters

STYLES AND TONES

When it comes to the style and tone of its responses, ChatGPT can exhibit a wide range of characteristics. Here's a comprehensive list of style and tone attributes that can be used with ChatGPT. Use each individually or combine a few (I'd say around three max) to see how they transform your output.

Academic: Writing that adheres to the conventions and standards of academia, often characterized by scholarly research and formal language.

Analytical: Writing that examines and breaks down a subject or issue, often focusing on logical reasoning and evidence.

Apathetic: Writing that is indifferent or lacking emotion, often with a focus on disinterest or detachment.

Apologetic: Writing that expresses regret, remorse, or apology for a mistake or offense.

Appreciative: Writing that expresses gratitude, recognition, or admiration for someone or something.

Argumentative: Writing that presents arguments or viewpoints with the intent to persuade or convince the reader.

Arousing: Writing that stimulates or excites the reader, often in a sensual manner.

Assertive: Writing that is confident, direct, and firm in expressing opinions or ideas.

Astonishing: Writing that is surprising or astounding, often with a focus on leaving the reader in awe.

Authoritative: Writing that demonstrates expertise, credibility, and a commanding tone.

Awkward: Writing that is uncomfortable or embarrassing, often with a focus on social or interpersonal situations.

Bold: Writing that is confident and fearless, often with a focus on taking risks or making a strong statement.

Captivating: Writing that holds the reader's attention and fascination, often through compelling storytelling or intriguing content.

Casual: Writing that is relaxed, informal, and conversational in tone.

Cautious: Writing that is careful, hesitant, or restrained in expressing opinions or making claims.

Clear: Writing that is easy to understand, concise, and unambiguous.

Collaborative: Writing that involves the input and perspectives of multiple individuals working together.

Comparative: Writing that compares and contrasts different aspects or elements, often highlighting similarities and differences.

Compassionate: Writing that shows empathy, understanding, and kindness towards others.

Concise: Writing that is clear, succinct, and to the point, often emphasizing brevity and efficiency.

Confident: Writing that exudes a sense of self-assurance and certainty, often with a focus on assertiveness or conviction.

Conversational: Writing that mimics a spoken conversation, often with a focus on engaging the reader in an informal, friendly manner.

Creative: Writing that showcases originality, imagination, and artistic expression, often exploring unique or unconventional ideas.

Critical: Writing that offers a detailed analysis or evaluation, often highlighting strengths, weaknesses, and potential improvements.

Curious: Writing that demonstrates a desire for knowledge, exploration, or inquiry.

Cynical: Writing that is skeptical or distrustful, often with a focus on questioning motives or challenging conventional wisdom.

Depictive: Writing that vividly portrays characters, scenes, or events through detailed descriptions.

Descriptive: Writing that vividly portrays people, places, objects, or events.

Direct: Writing that is straightforward, honest, and to the point.

Dramatic: Writing that is intense, emotional, or theatrical in nature.

Dreamy: Writing that evokes a sense of dreaming or imagination, often emphasizing surreal or ethereal elements.

Eerie: Writing that creates an unsettling or creepy atmosphere, often delving into the supernatural or unknown.

Elegant: Writing that exudes grace and refinement, often emphasizing beauty or sophistication.

Emotive: Writing that evokes strong emotions or feelings, often through vivid descriptions or personal anecdotes.

Emotional: Writing that evokes intense feelings or emotions in the reader.

Empathetic: Writing that demonstrates understanding, compassion, and the ability to identify with others' emotions or experiences.

Energetic: Writing that is full of vigor or enthusiasm, often with a focus on excitement or positivity.

Engaging: Writing that is compelling, intriguing, and effectively hooks the reader, making them eager to continue reading.

Entertaining: Writing that is enjoyable, amusing, and pleasurable to read.

Enthusiastic: Writing that is vibrant and full of energy, often emphasizing excitement or positivity.

Epic: Writing that encompasses grand tales of heroic adventures and legendary figures, weaving together epic events that captivate the imagination.

Evocative: Writing that elicits strong emotions, sensations, or memories in the reader.

Exhaustive: Writing that extensively covers a topic, leaving no aspect unexplored or unaddressed. It aims to provide thorough and comprehensive information, ensuring a comprehensive understanding of the subject.

Exhilarating: Writing that is exciting or invigorating, often with a focus on energy or enthusiasm.

Experimental: Writing that pushes boundaries or explores unconventional approaches, often challenging language or form.

Explanatory: Writing that serves the purpose of providing clear and understandable explanations or insights into a particular subject or topic.

Expository: Writing that explains, informs, or clarifies a topic or concept in a clear and concise manner.

Expressive: Writing that conveys emotions, feelings, or ideas with depth and intensity.

Fantastical: Writing that explores imaginative or magical elements, often set in fictional or fantastical worlds.

Figurative: Writing that employs figurative language, such as metaphors, similes, and symbolism, to convey deeper meanings and create vivid imagery that goes beyond literal interpretation.

Formal: Writing that adheres to established rules of grammar, style, and etiquette, often used in professional or academic settings.

Friendly: Writing that is warm, welcoming, and approachable in tone.

Heart-warming: Writing that evokes feelings of warmth or affection, often centered around positive emotions or relationships.

Heart-wrenching: Writing that evokes intense sadness or emotional pain, often with a focus on deeply moving or poignant moments.

Hilarious: Writing that is extremely funny or comedic, often with a focus on generating laughter.

Humorous: Writing that is intended to be funny or amusing, often employing wit, jokes, or comedic elements.

Imaginative: Writing that showcases creativity or imagination, often exploring unique or unconventional ideas.

Impersonal: Writing that is objective or detached, often focusing on impersonal subjects or concepts.

Informal: Writing that adopts a casual and relaxed style, using conversational language and a friendly tone. It deviates from strict formalities and allows for a more relaxed and accessible communication style, akin to a friendly conversation between acquaintances.

Informative: Writing that aims to provide knowledge or educate the reader.

Inspirational: Writing that aims to motivate or inspire the reader.

Intense: Writing that aims to be powerful or impactful, often leaving a strong emotional impression.

Introspective: Writing that encourages self-reflection and deep contemplation, often focusing on personal experiences or inner thoughts.

Joyful: Writing that evokes feelings of happiness or delight, often emphasizing positive experiences or emotions.

Legal: Writing that follows the established conventions and standards of the legal field, characterized by clarity, precision, and a focus on accurately interpreting and applying laws and regulations in a formal manner. It aims to convey legal information and arguments effectively to a specific audience, such as judges, attorneys, or legal professionals, using specialized terminology and a logical, organized structure.

Lighthearted: Writing that is playful or filled with levity, often using humor or fun to engage the reader.

Lyrical: Writing that is musical or poetic in nature, often emphasizing rhythm, imagery, and emotional expression.

Melancholic: Writing that evokes a sense of sadness or melancholy, often reflecting on introspection or contemplation.

Melodic: Writing that incorporates rhythm or musicality, often emphasizing language and sound.

Mournful: Writing that expresses feelings of sadness or loss, often centered around grief or sorrow.

Mysterious: Writing that is enigmatic or cryptic, often exploring secrecy or hidden meanings.

Narrative: Writing that brings stories to life, engaging readers with characters, events, and a compelling plot that unfolds with each turn of the page.

Nostalgic: Writing that evokes longing or nostalgia, often centered around the past or lost opportunities.

Opinionated: Writing that expresses strong personal opinions or biases on a particular topic.

Passionate: Writing that is full of energy and emotion, often reflecting personal beliefs or values.

Passionless: Writing that is devoid of strong emotions, often emphasizing factual information or objective analysis.

Pensive: Writing that is thoughtful and reflective, often with a focus on introspection or deep contemplation.

Personable: Writing that has a friendly, approachable, and relatable tone, creating a connection between the writer and the reader. It feels conversational and warm, as if the writer is speaking directly to the reader, fostering a sense of familiarity and personal connection.

Persuasive: Writing that seeks to convince the reader to take specific actions or adopt particular perspectives.

Philosophical: Writing that delves into deep questions and contemplations about existence, knowledge, values, and reality.

Playful: Writing that is light-hearted, fun, and full of playfulness.

Poetic: Writing that utilizes expressive and rhythmic language, often emphasizing imagery and emotion.

Powerful: Writing that is impactful or influential, often evoking strong emotions or intensity.

Professional: Writing that adheres to the standards and expectations of a particular profession or field.

Provocative: Writing that challenges or stimulates the reader, often presenting controversial or unconventional perspectives.

Realistic: Writing that accurately represents or reflects the real world, often portraying characters, events, or situations as they commonly occur.

Reflective: Writing that encourages introspection or contemplation, often centered around personal experiences or self-examination.

Revealing: Writing that discloses or unveils information, thoughts, or insights that were previously unknown or hidden.

Reverent: Writing that shows deep respect or admiration, often with a focus on sacred or spiritual themes.

Rhetorical: Writing that uses persuasive techniques and effective language to communicate and influence the reader.

Ridiculous: Writing that is absurd or laughable, often with a focus on exaggerated or silly elements.

Sarcastic: Writing that employs irony or mockery, often in a humorous manner.

Satirical: Writing that employs humor or irony to critique or ridicule something or someone.

Sensational: Writing that aims to shock or surprise the reader, often featuring dramatic or extraordinary events.

Sensitive: Writing that demonstrates sensitivity or empathy, often emphasizing understanding or inclusiveness.

Sensual: Writing that appeals to the senses and emotions, often emphasizing physical sensations or pleasure.

Serene: Writing that is calm and peaceful, often with a focus on tranquility or harmony.

Shocking: Writing that is startling or surprising, often aiming to provoke a strong reaction or challenge societal norms.

Simple: Writing that is uncomplicated, straightforward, and easy to understand.

Sincere: Writing that is genuine, honest, and heartfelt compassion.

Soothing: Writing that is calming or tranquil, often focusing on relaxation or serenity.

Sophisticated: Writing that is refined, cultured, and intellectually advanced.

Sorrowful: Writing that conveys a sense of sadness or melancholy, often focusing on feelings of grief or regret.

Spiritual: Writing that explores or delves into spiritual or metaphysical themes.

Storytelling: Writing that engages the reader through the art of storytelling, often with a narrative structure.

Straightforward: Writing that is clear, direct, and honest in conveying information or ideas.

Stream-of-consciousness: Writing that delves into the unfiltered and continuous flow of thoughts, emotions, and perceptions experienced by a character, offering a unique glimpse into their inner world.

Succinct: Writing that conveys information or ideas in a concise and precise manner, using minimal words yet effectively capturing the essence of the message.

Surprising: Writing that is unexpected or astonishing, often with a focus on creating a sense of wonder or amazement.

Suspenseful: Writing that builds anticipation or tension, often with a focus on creating a sense of mystery or anticipation.

Technical: Writing that is specialized and focused on conveying complex information or instructions with precision.

Thought-provoking: Writing that stimulates or prompts deep thinking, often raising challenging questions or ideas.

Thoughtful: Writing that encourages reflection or contemplation, often focusing on ideas or concepts.

Touching: Writing that elicits emotional or sentimental reactions, often evoking empathy or sympathy.

Unapologetic: Writing that is bold, confident, and unapologetic in its beliefs or actions.

Unconventional: Writing that deviates from traditional or expected norms, often exploring new ideas or approaches.

Unique: Writing that is distinctive, individual, and stands out from the ordinary or commonplace.

Unpredictable: Writing that is full of surprises or unexpected twists and turns.

Uplifting: Writing that instills a sense of positivity or inspiration, often focusing on hope or optimism.

Vibrant: Writing that is lively, energetic, and full of vitality.

Vivacious: Writing that is lively, vibrant, and full of energy, often with a focus on vivacity and exuberance.

Vivid: Writing that is rich in detail and imagery, often painting a clear and vibrant picture in the reader's mind.

Whimsical: Writing that is fanciful, quaint, or playful, often exploring imagination or fantasy.

Witty: Writing that is clever, humorous, and quick-witted.

Wonder-filled: Writing that inspires a sense of wonder or amazement, often evoking curiosity or awe.

Zany: Writing that is eccentric or unconventional, often characterized by wild or unpredictable humor.

Zealous: Writing that is filled with passionate enthusiasm or fervor, often reflecting intense dedication or commitment.

Zen-like: Writing that embodies a state of calmness and tranquility, often drawing inspiration from Zen philosophy or meditation.

Zestful: Writing that is full of energy and enthusiasm, often with a focus on liveliness and vitality.

Tip 1: You can also train ChatGPT to mimic your very own style and tone. I've used this on many occasions including for quickly answering emails in a way that preserved my style and tone.

> **Prompt:** Analyze the following text for style and tone. Apply that exact style and tone to all future responses.
>
> [Add a sample of your writing, could be several emails, a blog post, essay, just whatever you have available]
>
> **Prompt:** Write a 300-word blog post on 10 simple methods for organizing your home and reducing clutter

Tip 2: Use the above command to mimic the style and tone of your favorite website, pasting in a few paragraphs from that particular site instead.

Tip 3:

> **Prompt:** Write a 100-word blog post on 10 simple methods for organizing your home and reducing clutter at a 5th grade reading level

Tip 4:

> **Prompt:** Write a 100-word blog on 10 simple methods for organizing your home and reducing clutter in style of [your favorite author or person]

Tip 5:

> **Prompt:** Tell a joke about electricians and light bulbs in the voice of [Eddie Murphy]
>
> Now substitute Eddie Murphy for Ricky Gervais, Bill Burr, and Kevin Hart. I must admit ChatGPT had me laughing out loud on this one!

*** Note:** These commands will only work within that particular (or specific) chat the prompt was invoked in.

STRUCTURES AND FORMATS

Although ChatGPT replies to prompts in plain text language, it has built-in features that allow you to fine-tune its output to just about any format or structure you'd like (within reason). The following prompts will give you an idea of the model's capabilities.

Alphabetical order
Prompt: Create an alphabetized list of all the main parts found on a computer

Blockquote
Prompt: Write a blockquote expressing a famous quote by Albert Einstein

Bold
Prompt: Write a sentence in bold to emphasize the importance of teamwork

Bullet points
Prompt: Create a bulleted list of the benefits of regular exercise

Checklist
Prompt: Create a checklist of tasks for planning a child's birthday party

Code
Prompt: [Desired code or function] in [programming language]
Prompt: Create a countdown timer in JavaScript

Comma-separated values (CSV)
Prompt: Show me an example of the CSV file format

Dialogue
Prompt: Suggest dialogue for a scene in which a start up founder gets stuck on an elevator with a potential investor

A different language:
Prompt: Give me the French equivalent for "Hello, how are you today?"

Emoji's
Prompt: Add emojis to this: I had a wonderful time on my vacation at the beach in Gulf Shores!

Graph
Prompt: Create a graph to represent the monthly sales figures for a product

Hashtags
Prompt: Add popular hashtags to this: I had a wonderful time on my vacation at the beach in Gulf Shores!

Heading
Prompt: Can you display the heading format for me?

HTML
Prompt: Generate 3 HTML-formatted paragraphs about the benefits of exercise combined into a single output

Prompt: Generate 3 HTML-formatted paragraphs about the benefits of exercise combined into a single output. Use heading, subheadings, bullet points, and bold to organize the information

Italics
Prompt: Write an italicized sentence describing the tranquility of a peaceful garden

JSON
Prompt: Convert the following data into JSON format: name: John, age: 30, city: New York

Nested list
Prompt: Create a nested list outlining the steps to make a delicious pizza

Numbered list
Prompt: Create a numbered list of steps to follow for effective time management

Outline
Prompt: Provide an outline for an article on the pros and cons of using ChatGPT

PowerPoint
Prompt: Give me an example of the Microsoft PowerPoint presentation format

Python
Prompt: Write a Python function to calculate the factorial of a number

Question and answer format
Prompt: Give me 10 questions and answers using the Q and A format on questions I may be asked during a UX interview

Sequential instructions or step-by-step
Prompt: How can I make banana pudding? Give me a step-by-step guide

Social media ready (ChatGPT automatically generates content in the required platform length or desired time frame)

Prompt: Create a LinkedIn post on why content designers should familiarize themselves with ChatGPT

Prompt: Compose a tweet advertising this article

Prompt: Now create a 2 minute YouTube script. Provide approximate timing for each section

Table

Prompt: Create a table that compares the features of different electric vehicles

Unordered list

Prompt: Create an unordered list of steps to follow for effective time management

Yaml (dataset)/ Extensible Markup Language (XML)

Prompt: You have a dataset containing information about products in an e-commerce store. Convert the dataset into XML format and provide an example of the resulting XML document

Tip 1: Show or tell ChatGPT exactly how you want the output formatted.

> **Prompt:** Provide the capitals of the following countries Germany, England, Italy, Australia, Brazil, Canada, and India using this the format: The capital of USA is Washington
>
> **Prompt:** Write 5 attention grabbing headlines for a blog post on prompt engineering with ChatGPT. Include emojis at the end of every headline. Use title case in each headline and provide a list of hashtags at the end of each

Tip 2: Explore different narrative modes with ChatGPT

> **Prompt:** Write 3 very short paragraphs on a first visit to Rome in the first, second, and third person

RANDOM "INBETWEENERS"

The more you interact with ChatGPT, the more you'll come to realize that you really can just "talk to it" using natural language and phrasing, just as you do in your everyday conversations. Consider this tiny section a catch-all for simple yet effective prompts that can be used at different stages throughout your conversations that will serve to greatly enhance your interactions.

- Continue
- More
- 5 more
- Expand on [subject]
- Provide more detail
- Make it longer
- Make it easier to read
- Make it easier to understand
- Be as specific as possible
- Explain [topic] in simple terms
- Explain the above in 1 sentence
- Rewrite that in 1 sentence
- Show me what changes you made
- Summarize this paragraph into bullet points
- Summarize and extract key findings and insights from this [text]
- What are 5 key takeaways from this
- Give constructive feedback on the following
- Improve this writing and optimize for higher conversion [text]
- What are 5 ways I can improve this [text]
- Tailor your answer to [target audience]
- Include accurate statistics and industry data (always fact check)
- Increase credibility by adding quotes from experts or influential figures (another fact check alert)

- Suggest some hacks for [subject]
- [Prompt task or question] Let's think step by step
- [End of prompt command when priming (if necessary)]. Do not write explanations or replies.
- [Whatever your prompt is] Do you understand?
- Restart (Allows you to start fresh within an ongoing conversation, providing you with a clean slate to continue the discussion. This can be helpful if you want to change the direction or context of the conversation without having to start a completely new chat session.)

Chapter 5: A Few Additional Tips on ChatGPT

Before we get to the UX prompts presented in the next chapter, let's take a moment to consider a few additional tips about ChatGPT you should keep in mind.

ChatGPT is extremely venerable to input phrasing, meaning that the phrasing and wording of a question or prompt can significantly impact ChatGPT's response. Minor rephrasing may lead to different or contradictory answers. This sensitivity to input phrasing makes the model less robust and inconsistent in providing reliable information.

Another important thing to understand is "Prompt drift." Prompt drift is when an AI language model starts to behave differently or give outputs that are different from what was initially intended, deviating from the original context or instructions given to the model. Prompt drift may be a result of the model's tendency to generate creative or imaginative responses rather than sticking strictly to the prompt which can lead to unexpected or nonsensical outputs that may not align with your expectations. This is an ongoing challenge in AI development.

Also, as previously discussed in chapter 2, at times ChatGPT may "hallucinate" and just simply make stuff up (potentially providing incorrect information about individuals, locations, or facts). For this reason I cannot stress enough the importance of verifying all information generated by ChatGPT to ensure accuracy. Consult fact-checking websites like Snopes, Factcheck, PolitiFact, BBC Reality Check, The Washington Post Fact Checker, The New York Times Fact Check, AP Fact Check, Reuters Fact Check–to name a few.

Lastly, it's worth mentioning that, as of the time of this writing (and as I just found out), there is no way for you to recover mistakenly deleted chats. UGH! So fair warning that if you come up with something amazing (and I have no doubt you will) back it up somewhere, somehow–either by copying and pasting or through the export function found hidden under settings. Now that's all out the way, let's get to these prompts!

NOTE: As an additional benefit of purchasing this book, all prompts are available for free download from: www.uxwithchatgpt.com. Make sure to remember the last word from the paragraph above as you'll need it for the download. (Hint: It's plural and does not include the exclamation.)

Chapter 6: Prompts for UX'ers

In the words of Lisa Stansfield "Been around the world and I, I, I"...well you're finally here–the part you've been eagerly anticipating. I guarantee you'll find these UX focused prompts to be super useful no matter what your role. Intended to spark ideas and provide inspiration, they will only serve to inform, educate, and enhance whatever it is you do on a daily basis.

Know that using all the elements found in my formula is NOT at all necessary. You may want to start with just a simple task or question and go from there. The prompts are literally packed with information, so experiment. Pick, choose, add, remove, combine, change the order of elements–just get creative, making sure to note how your changes affect the given output. These prompts are somewhat generic in nature. To truly unlock their power, prime them first with information that describes your particular scenario or need and fine-tune from there.

As any UX'er will know, the following role definitions are not set in stone. Duties typically overlap and responsibilities will differ based on factors such as the industry, the specific product or service being offered, the size and maturity of the company, and, of course, your own level of expertise or experience. Nevertheless, these descriptions will help to understand the underlying intent behind the prompts found in each category. Go through them all–it's very likely a UX writer will find a helpful prompt within the UX researcher section and vica versa.

Content Designer: A content designer is responsible for creating and structuring content that is user-centered and supports the overall user experience. They work closely with designers and developers to ensure that the content is presented effectively and meets the users' needs.

Information Architect: An information architect focuses on organizing and structuring information in a way that is intuitive and user-friendly. They analyze user research, conduct content audits, and create sitemaps and wireframes to establish the navigation and structure of a digital product.

UX Writer: A UX writer specializes in creating clear, concise, and engaging copy that guides users through a digital product or interface. They collaborate closely with designers and researchers to ensure that the words used in the product are user-centric, consistent, and aligned with the brand's voice.

Copywriter: A copywriter is responsible for crafting persuasive and compelling copy for marketing materials, product descriptions, and other promotional content. They work closely with the marketing team to develop messaging strategies that resonate with the target audience.

UX Editor: A UX editor is responsible for reviewing and refining the written content within a digital product or interface. They ensure consistency in style, tone, and messaging, and may also collaborate with UX writers to improve the overall quality of the content.

Conversational Designer: A conversational designer focuses on designing conversational interfaces such as chatbots and voice assistants. They create dialogue flows, write dialogue scripts, and ensure that the interactions between users and the system are natural, intuitive, and user-friendly.

Content Strategist: A content strategist develops and implements a strategic plan for creating and managing content across various platforms and touchpoints. They work closely with UX writers, designers, and stakeholders to align content goals with user needs and business objectives.

Accessibility Writer: An accessibility writer specializes in creating content that is accessible and inclusive to all users. They ensure that content meets accessibility guidelines and standards, including providing alternative text for images, using clear and concise language, and considering different user needs allowing all users to access and understand the information effectively.

Documentation Writer: A documentation writer creates user manuals, help guides, and other documentation to assist users in understanding and using a product. They have strong technical writing skills and are able to explain complex concepts in a clear and concise manner.

Technical Writer: A technical writer creates documentation and instructional materials that explain complex technical concepts or processes. They collaborate with developers and subject matter experts to gather information and translate it into user-friendly content, examples include API documentation and user guides.

Product Designer: A product designer is responsible for the end-to-end design process of a product, collaborating with cross-functional teams to create innovative and user-centered solutions. They conduct user research, define product goals, and create wireframes and prototypes to gather feedback. Product designers focus on usability and aesthetics, considering details like typography and visual hierarchy. They iterate on designs based on user feedback, aiming to deliver products that meet user needs while aligning with business objectives. By combining creativity, user insights, and technical knowledge, product designers create compelling and user-friendly products that provide a delightful user experience.

UX Researcher: A UX researcher gathers and analyzes user insights to inform the design of digital products. They use various research methods to collect data on user behavior, needs, and motivations, identifying opportunities for improvement. By collaborating with stakeholders and designers, UX researchers shape the direction of the product based on user feedback, ensuring user-centered experiences that perfectly align with business goals.

Prompts for Content Designers

1.

[Role]: Content Designer
[Task]: Conduct user research to inform content creation for a new product feature.
[Context]: Understanding user needs, preferences, and pain points.
[Goal]: Develop user-focused content that resonates with the target audience.
[Constraints]: Utilize qualitative and quantitative research methods.
[Style or Tone]: Empathetic, engaging, and persuasive.
[Structure or Format]: Prepared user research findings report and content recommendations.

Prompt: As a Content Designer, conduct user research to inform content creation for a new product feature. The goal is to develop user-focused content that resonates with the target audience. Please utilize qualitative and quantitative research methods, using an empathetic, engaging, and persuasive style. Provide a prepared user research findings report and content recommendations.

2.

[Role]: Content Designer
[Task]: Write concise and persuasive landing page copy for a mobile app promoting healthy eating habits.
[Context]: The landing page will target health-conscious individuals.
[Goal]: Highlight the app's features, benefits, and impact on users' well-being.
[Constraints]: Maintain a friendly and motivating tone.
[Style or Tone]: Friendly, motivating, and aligned with the target audience.
[Structure or Format]: Compelling copy with clear call-to-action.

Prompt: As a Content Designer, write concise and persuasive landing page copy for a mobile app promoting healthy eating habits. The goal is to highlight the app's features, benefits, and impact on users' well-being. Please maintain a friendly and motivating tone that aligns with the target audience. Provide compelling copy with a clear call-to-action.

3.

[Role]: Content Designer
[Task]: Create user journey maps to visualize the end-to-end user experience.
[Context]: Understanding user interactions and touchpoints with a product or service.
[Goal]: Identify pain points, opportunities, and areas for improvement.
[Constraints]: Conduct user research and map user interactions and emotions.
[Style or Tone]: Visual, storytelling, and user-centric.
[Structure or Format]: Prepared user journey maps, illustrating key touchpoints and user emotions.

Prompt: As a Content Designer, create user journey maps to visualize the end-to-end user experience. The goal is to identify pain points, opportunities, and areas for improvement. Please conduct user research and map user interactions and emotions, using a visual, storytelling, and user-centric style. Provide prepared user journey maps, illustrating key touchpoints and user emotions.

4.
[Role]: Content Designer
[Task]: Craft engaging and informative email newsletters for a nonprofit organization.
[Context]: The newsletters will update donors and supporters on the organization's initiatives.
[Goal]: Inspire action, share success stories, and provide opportunities for involvement.
[Constraints]: Align with the organization's mission and maintain a warm and compelling tone.
[Style or Tone]: Warm, compelling, and aligned with the organization's mission.
[Structure or Format]: Well-structured newsletters with impactful content.

Prompt: As a Content Designer, craft engaging and informative email newsletters for a nonprofit organization. The goal is to inspire action, share success stories, and provide opportunities for involvement. Please align with the organization's mission and maintain a warm and compelling tone. Provide well-structured newsletters with impactful content.

5.
[Role]: Content Designer
[Task]: Conduct a content audit to assess the effectiveness of existing website content.
[Context]: Evaluating content performance and identifying areas for improvement.

[Goal]: Enhance user experience, readability, and information accessibility.
[Constraints]: Analyze existing content across multiple webpages.
[Style or Tone]: Analytical, thorough, and data-driven.
[Structure or Format]: Prepared content audit report with recommendations.

Prompt: As a Content Designer, conduct a content audit to assess the effectiveness of existing website content. The goal is to enhance user experience, readability, and information accessibility. Please analyze existing content across multiple webpages, using an analytical, thorough, and data-driven approach. Provide a prepared content audit report with recommendations.

6.

[Role]: Content Designer
[Task]: Develop a content style guide for a fashion e-commerce platform.
[Context]: The style guide will govern tone, language, and formatting across different content types.
[Goal]: Ensure consistency in brand communication.
[Constraints]: Align with the fashion e-commerce platform's brand.
[Style or Tone]: Visually appealing and easy to reference.
[Structure or Format]: Detailed guidelines for tone, language, and formatting.

Prompt: As a Content Designer, develop a content style guide for a fashion e-commerce platform. The goal is to ensure consistency in brand communication. Please ensure the style guide aligns with the fashion e-commerce platform's brand and provides detailed guidelines for tone, language, and formatting in a visually appealing and easy-to-reference format.

7.

[Role]: Content Designer
[Task]: Write compelling and informative product descriptions for a home decor e-commerce website.
[Context]: The descriptions will highlight the unique features, benefits, and craftsmanship of each product.
[Goal]: Maintain a consistent brand voice while enticing customers to make purchases.
[Constraints]: Provide descriptions in short paragraphs with bullet points for key details.
[Style or Tone]: Descriptive, persuasive, and aligned with the brand voice.
[Structure or Format]: Short paragraphs with bullet points for key details.

Prompt: As a Content Designer, write compelling and informative product descriptions for a home decor e-commerce website. The goal is to maintain a consistent brand voice while enticing customers to make purchases. Please provide descriptions in short paragraphs with bullet points for key details, using a descriptive, persuasive tone aligned with the brand voice.

8.

[Role]: Content Designer
[Task]: Create clear and user-friendly error messages for a mobile banking app.
[Context]: The messages will communicate errors, provide guidance, and assure users of the app's security.
[Goal]: Use a concise and empathetic tone within the limited space for error messages.
[Constraints]: Consider the limitations of space for error messages.
[Style or Tone]: Concise, empathetic, and reassuring.
[Structure or Format]: Example error messages for different scenarios.

Prompt: As a Content Designer, create clear and user-friendly error messages for a mobile banking app. The goal is to use a concise and empathetic tone within the limited space for error messages. Please consider the limitations of space and provide example error messages for different scenarios.

9.

[Role]: Content Designer
[Task]: Develop a content calendar for a social media platform targeting fitness enthusiasts.
[Context]: The calendar will include motivational quotes, informative articles, and interactive content.
[Goal]: Engage and inspire fitness enthusiasts.
[Constraints]: Align with the platform's branding, business goals, and SEO best practices.
[Style or Tone]: Exciting, informative, and visually appealing.
[Structure or Format]: Well-organized content calendar with specific topics and dates.

Prompt: As a Content Designer, develop a content calendar for a social media platform targeting fitness enthusiasts. The goal is to engage and inspire fitness enthusiasts. Please align the content calendar with the platform's branding, business goals, and SEO best practices. Provide a well-organized content calendar with specific topics and dates.

10.

[Role]: Content Designer
[Task]: Write alternative text descriptions for images on an e-learning platform.
[Context]: The descriptions will enable visually impaired learners to comprehend the content.
[Goal]: Provide accurate and descriptive alternative text descriptions.

[Constraints]: Balance conciseness with providing sufficient information for understanding.
[Style or Tone]: Clear, descriptive, and inclusive.
[Structure or Format]: Example alternative text descriptions for different types of images.

Prompt: As a Content Designer, write alternative text descriptions for images on an e-learning platform. The goal is to provide accurate and descriptive alternative text descriptions for visually impaired learners to comprehend the content. Please balance conciseness with providing sufficient information for understanding. Provide example alternative text descriptions for different types of images.

11.
[Role]: Content Designer
[Task]: Develop a content strategy for an email marketing campaign.
[Context]: Planning and executing email campaigns to engage subscribers.
[Goal]: Increase open rates, click-through rates, and conversions.
[Constraints]: Consider audience segmentation, A/B testing, and email best practices.
[Style or Tone]: Persuasive, compelling, and personalized.
[Structure or Format]: Prepared content strategy document and email templates.

Prompt: As a Content Designer, develop a content strategy for an email marketing campaign. The goal is to increase open rates, click-through rates, and conversions. Please consider audience segmentation, A/B testing, and email best practices, using a persuasive, compelling, and personalized style. Provide a prepared content strategy document and email templates.

12.

[Role]: Content Designer
[Task]: Develop user-centered microcopy for a mobile app's onboarding process.
[Context]: The microcopy will guide users through various app features.
[Goal]: Provide clear instructions and minimize user confusion.
[Constraints]: Limited space for each microcopy.
[Style or Tone]: Concise, friendly, and action-oriented.
[Structure or Format]: Examples of onboarding microcopy for different app features.

Prompt: As a Content Designer, develop user-centered microcopy for a mobile app's onboarding process. The goal is to provide clear instructions and minimize user confusion while guiding users through various app features. Please ensure the microcopy is concise, friendly, and action-oriented. Provide examples of onboarding microcopy for different app features.

13.

[Role]: Content Designer
[Task]: Write engaging social media captions for a travel company's Instagram account.
[Context]: The captions will accompany stunning travel photographs.
[Goal]: Spark curiosity and inspire travel aspirations.
[Constraints]: Limited character count for each caption.
[Style or Tone]: Captivating, adventurous, and visually descriptive.
[Structure or Format]: Example social media captions for different travel destinations.

Prompt: As a Content Designer, write engaging social media captions for a travel company's Instagram account. The goal is to spark curiosity and inspire travel aspirations through captivating, adventurous, and visually descriptive captions accompanying stunning travel photographs. Please consider the limited character count for each caption and provide examples for different travel destinations.

14.

[Role]: Content Designer
[Task]: Develop a content strategy for a software company's blog.
[Context]: The blog aims to establish the company as a thought leader in the industry.
[Goal]: Provide valuable insights, tips, and industry updates to readers.
[Constraints]: Align with the company's brand identity and target audience.
[Style or Tone]: Informative, authoritative, and industry-relevant.
[Structure or Format]: Content strategy outline with topic clusters and key focus areas.

Prompt: As a Content Designer, develop a content strategy for a software company's blog. The goal is to establish the company as a thought leader in the industry by providing valuable insights, tips, and industry updates to readers. Please ensure alignment with the company's brand identity and target audience. Provide a content strategy outline with topic clusters and key focus areas.

15.

[Role]: Content Designer
[Task]: Collaborate with UX team to develop content guidelines for a website redesign.
[Context]: Updating and refreshing website content for improved user experience.
[Goal]: Ensure consistency, clarity, and alignment with brand voice.
[Constraints]: Work within the existing design framework and maintain SEO best practices.
[Style or Tone]: Consistent, informative, and brand-aligned.
[Structure or Format]: Prepared content style guide and recommendations.

Prompt: As a Content Designer, collaborate with the UX team to develop content guidelines for a website redesign. The goal is to ensure consistency, clarity, and alignment with the brand voice. Please work within the existing design framework and maintain SEO best practices, using a consistent, informative, and brand-aligned style. Provide a prepared content style guide and recommendations.

16.

[Role]: Content Designer
[Task]: Create a user-friendly and informative FAQ page for an e-commerce website.
[Context]: The FAQ page will address common customer queries and provide solutions.
[Goal]: Help customers find answers quickly and reduce support requests.
[Constraints]: Use concise and clear language to address each question.
[Style or Tone]: Informative, helpful, and easy to understand.
[Structure or Format]: Well-organized FAQ page with categorized questions and answers.

Prompt: As a Content Designer, create a user-friendly and informative FAQ page for an e-commerce website. The goal is to help customers find answers quickly and reduce support requests by addressing common customer queries and providing solutions. Please use concise and clear language to address each question and provide a well-organized FAQ page with categorized questions and answers.

17.

[Role]: Content Designer
[Task]: Develop a content template for product descriptions on an online marketplace.
[Context]: The template will be used by sellers to create consistent and compelling descriptions.
[Goal]: Highlight product features, specifications, and unique selling points.

[Constraints]: Provide sections for key details and maintain consistency.
[Style or Tone]: Engaging, persuasive, and aligned with the target audience.
[Structure or Format]: Content template with sections for key details and persuasive elements.

Prompt: As a Content Designer, develop a content template for product descriptions on an online marketplace. The goal is to help sellers create consistent and compelling descriptions that highlight product features, specifications, and unique selling points. Please provide sections for key details and maintain consistency in an engaging, persuasive tone. Provide a content template with sections for key details and persuasive elements.

18.
[Role]: Content Designer
[Task]: Create a content calendar for a social media marketing campaign.
[Context]: Planning and organizing content for social media platforms.
[Goal]: Maintain a consistent and engaging social media presence.
[Constraints]: Adhere to brand guidelines and target audience preferences.
[Style or Tone]: Creative, conversational, and on-brand.
[Structure or Format]: Prepared content calendar with post ideas and schedules.

Prompt: As a Content Designer, create a content calendar for a social media marketing campaign. The goal is to maintain a consistent and engaging social media presence. Please adhere to brand guidelines and target audience preferences, using a creative, conversational, and on-brand style. Provide a prepared content calendar with post ideas and schedules.

19.
[Role]: Content Designer
[Task]: Develop a content plan for a social media campaign promoting a charity event.

[Context]: The campaign aims to increase event attendance and donations.
[Goal]: Create excitement, highlight the event's impact, and encourage participation.
[Constraints]: Align with the charity's brand voice and campaign timeline.
[Style or Tone]: Inspiring, compassionate, and action-oriented.
[Structure or Format]: Content plan with specific posts, captions, and visuals for the campaign.

Prompt: As a Content Designer, develop a content plan for a social media campaign promoting a charity event. The goal is to create excitement, highlight the event's impact, and encourage participation by aligning with the charity's brand voice and campaign timeline. Please provide a content plan with specific posts, captions, and visuals for the campaign.

20.
[Role]: Content Designer
[Task]: Collaborate with UI designers to create visually appealing content layouts.
[Context]: Integrating content and design elements for seamless user experience.
[Goal]: Enhance content presentation and engagement.
[Constraints]: Work within the given design framework and design principles.
[Style or Tone]: Harmonious, balanced, and aesthetically pleasing.
[Structure or Format]: Prepared content layout prototypes and design guidelines.

Prompt: As a Content Designer, collaborate with UI designers to create visually appealing content layouts. The goal is to enhance content presentation and engagement. Please work within the given design framework and design principles, using a harmonious, balanced, and aesthetically pleasing style. Provide prepared content layout prototypes and design guidelines.

21.

[Role]: Content Designer
[Task]: Develop a style guide for a fashion brand's blog.
[Context]: The style guide will ensure consistency in tone, voice, and formatting.
[Goal]: Establish a cohesive brand identity and enhance readability.
[Constraints]: Consider the target audience and align with the brand's values.
[Style or Tone]: Consistent, on-brand, and accessible.
[Structure or Format]: Style guide document with guidelines for tone, voice, and formatting.

Prompt: As a Content Designer, develop a style guide for a fashion brand's blog. The goal is to establish a cohesive brand identity and enhance readability by providing guidelines for tone, voice, and formatting. Please consider the target audience and align the style guide with the brand's values. Provide a style guide document with clear guidelines.

22.

[Role]: Content Designer
[Task]: Write informative and user-friendly product documentation for a software application.
[Context]: The documentation will help users understand the application's features and functionalities.
[Goal]: Provide comprehensive guidance and troubleshooting information.
[Constraints]: Use clear language and organize the documentation into sections or chapters.
[Style or Tone]: Clear, concise, and user-oriented.
[Structure or Format]: Well-organized product documentation with table of contents and step-by-step instructions.

Prompt: As a Content Designer, write informative and user-friendly product documentation for a software application. The goal is to provide comprehensive guidance and troubleshooting information to help users understand the application's features and functionalities. Please use clear language and organize the documentation into sections or chapters. Provide well-organized product documentation with a table of contents and step-by-step instructions.

23.

[Role]: Content Designer
[Task]: Create compelling and concise headlines for a news website's articles.
[Context]: The headlines will attract readers' attention and accurately represent the article content.
[Goal]: Increase click-through rates and engage readers.
[Constraints]: Use limited characters while conveying the article's main message.
[Style or Tone]: Captivating, informative, and aligned with the news website's style.
[Structure or Format]: Example headlines for different types of news articles.

Prompt: As a Content Designer, create compelling and concise headlines for a news website's articles. The goal is to increase click-through rates and engage readers by attracting their attention and accurately representing the article content. Please use limited characters while conveying the article's main message and provide example headlines for different types of news articles.

24.

[Role]: Content Designer
[Task]: Develop a content plan for an educational institution's blog.
[Context]: The blog aims to provide valuable information and resources for students and parents.

[Goal]: Establish the institution as a trusted educational resource.
[Constraints]: Align with the institution's branding and educational objectives.
[Style or Tone]: Informative, authoritative, and student-friendly.
[Structure or Format]: Content plan with specific topics, target audience, and publishing schedule.

Prompt: As a Content Designer, develop a content plan for an educational institution's blog. The goal is to establish the institution as a trusted educational resource by providing valuable information and resources for students and parents. Please align the content plan with the institution's branding and educational objectives, and include specific topics, target audience, and a publishing schedule.

25.
[Role]: Content Designer
[Task]: Create user-centered content for a mobile app onboarding process.
[Context]: Guiding users through the initial setup and introduction to the app.
[Goal]: Enhance user understanding, engagement, and successful adoption.
[Constraints]: Limited space, attention, and the need for clear instructions.
[Style or Tone]: Concise, friendly, and informative.
[Structure or Format]: Prepared onboarding content scripts and visual layouts.

Prompt: As a Content Designer, create user-centered content for a mobile app onboarding process. The goal is to enhance user understanding, engagement, and successful adoption. Please consider the limited space, attention, and the need for clear instructions, using a concise, friendly, and informative style. Provide prepared onboarding content scripts and visual layouts.

Prompts for Information Architects

1.

[Role]: Information Architect
[Task]: Conduct a thorough content audit of a company's website.
[Context]: The website contains numerous pages with varying content types.
[Goal]: Assess the quality, relevance, and organization of the existing content.
[Constraints]: Consider the website's target audience and business objectives.
[Style or Tone]: Analytical, detailed, and objective.
[Structure or Format]: Content audit report with findings and recommendations.

Prompt: As an Information Architect, conduct a thorough content audit of a company's website. The goal is to assess the quality, relevance, and organization of the existing content. Please consider the website's target audience and business objectives. Provide a content audit report with detailed findings and recommendations.

2.

[Role]: Information Architect
[Task]: Create a sitemap for a large e-commerce website.
[Context]: The website has multiple product categories and subcategories.
[Goal]: Visualize the website's hierarchical structure and navigation flow.
[Constraints]: Consider user experience and ease of navigation.
[Style or Tone]: Visual, organized, and user-centered.
[Structure or Format]: Sitemap diagram or visual representation.

Prompt: As an Information Architect, create a sitemap for a large e-commerce website. The goal is to visualize the website's hierarchical structure and navigation flow. Please consider user experience and ease of navigation. Provide a sitemap diagram or visual representation.

3.

[Role]: Information Architect
[Task]: Define and implement a taxonomy system for a large knowledge base.
[Context]: Structuring and categorizing information for easy navigation and retrieval.
[Goal]: Improve searchability and findability of content.
[Constraints]: Consistency with industry standards and user mental models.
[Style or Tone]: Clear, concise, and hierarchical.
[Structure or Format]: Prepared taxonomy framework and classification guidelines.

Prompt: As an Information Architect, define and implement a taxonomy system for a large knowledge base. The goal is to improve searchability and findability of content. Please ensure consistency with industry standards and user mental models, using a clear, concise, and hierarchical style. Provide a prepared taxonomy framework and classification guidelines.

4.

[Role]: Information Architect
[Task]: Conduct a content inventory and organize information for a website redesign.
[Context]: Assessing existing content and reimagining its structure for improved usability.
[Goal]: Create an intuitive and user-friendly information architecture.
[Constraints]: Consider user needs, business goals, and technical requirements.
[Style or Tone]: Systematic, logical, and user-centric.

[Structure or Format]: Prepared site map and content organization guidelines.

Prompt: As an Information Architect, conduct a content inventory and organize information for a website redesign. The goal is to create an intuitive and user-friendly information architecture. Please consider user needs, business goals, and technical requirements, using a systematic, logical, and user-centric approach. Provide a prepared site map and content organization guidelines.

5.
[Role]: Information Architect
[Task]: Conduct a card sorting exercise to determine optimal menu categories.
[Context]: The exercise will involve a representative sample of users.
[Goal]: Create a user-centered and intuitive website navigation structure.
[Constraints]: Use appropriate card sorting techniques and analysis.
[Style or Tone]: Collaborative, user-focused, and evidence-based.
[Structure or Format]: Card sorting report with results and recommendations.

Prompt: As an Information Architect, conduct a card sorting exercise to determine optimal menu categories for a website. The goal is to create a user-centered and intuitive navigation structure. Please use appropriate card sorting techniques and analysis. Provide a card sorting report with results and recommendations.

6.
[Role]: Information Architect
[Task]: Define metadata standards for a digital asset management system.
[Context]: The system will store various types of media files.
[Goal]: Ensure consistency and findability of digital assets.
[Constraints]: Consider industry standards and best practices.

[Style or Tone]: Technical, precise, and comprehensive.
[Structure or Format]: Metadata standards document with definitions and guidelines.

Prompt: As an Information Architect, define metadata standards for a digital asset management system. The goal is to ensure consistency and findability of digital assets. Please consider industry standards and best practices. Provide a metadata standards document with clear definitions and guidelines.

7.
[Role]: Information Architect
[Task]: Conduct a usability evaluation of a website's information architecture.
[Context]: The evaluation will involve user testing and feedback.
[Goal]: Identify usability issues and recommend improvements.
[Constraints]: Use appropriate usability evaluation methods and metrics.
[Style or Tone]: Objective, evaluative, and action-oriented.
[Structure or Format]: Usability evaluation report with findings and recommendations.

Prompt: As an Information Architect, conduct a usability evaluation of a website's information architecture. The goal is to identify usability issues and recommend improvements. Please use appropriate usability evaluation methods and metrics. Provide a usability evaluation report with findings and recommendations.

8.
[Role]: Information Architect
[Task]: Design an intuitive search interface for a complex database.
[Context]: The database contains a large volume of structured data.
[Goal]: Enable users to easily search and retrieve specific information.

[Constraints]: Consider user needs and database structure.
[Style or Tone]: User-friendly, efficient, and visually appealing.
[Structure or Format]: Search interface prototype or wireframe.

Prompt: As an Information Architect, design an intuitive search interface for a complex database. The goal is to enable users to easily search and retrieve specific information. Please consider user needs and the database structure. Provide a search interface prototype or wireframe.

9.
[Role]: Information Architect
[Task]: Conduct a content gap analysis to identify missing or outdated information on a website.
[Context]: Evaluating content coverage and relevance to user needs.
[Goal]: Ensure comprehensive and up-to-date content for a better user experience.
[Constraints]: Limited resources and time for content creation and updates.
[Style or Tone]: Analytical, research-oriented, and action-oriented.
[Structure or Format]: Prepared content gap analysis report with recommendations.

Prompt: As an Information Architect, conduct a content gap analysis to identify missing or outdated information on a website. The goal is to ensure comprehensive and up-to-date content for a better user experience. Please consider the limited resources and time for content creation and updates, using an analytical, research-oriented, and action-oriented approach. Provide a prepared content gap analysis report with recommendations.

10.
[Role]: Information Architect
[Task]: Conduct a user journey mapping exercise for an e-commerce website.

[Context]: The exercise will involve understanding user interactions and touchpoints.
[Goal]: Identify pain points and opportunities for enhancing the user experience.
[Constraints]: Use appropriate visualization techniques and customer insights.
[Style or Tone]: User-centric, holistic, and actionable.
[Structure or Format]: User journey map diagram or visualization.

Prompt: As an Information Architect, conduct a user journey mapping exercise for an e-commerce website. The goal is to identify pain points and opportunities for enhancing the user experience by understanding user interactions and touchpoints. Please use appropriate visualization techniques and customer insights. Provide a user journey map diagram or visualization.

11.
[Role]: Information Architect
[Task]: Develop a data classification scheme for a large enterprise.
[Context]: The scheme will encompass various types of sensitive data.
[Goal]: Ensure data security and compliance with regulations.
[Constraints]: Consider industry standards and privacy requirements.
[Style or Tone]: Methodical, precise, and secure.
[Structure or Format]: Data classification scheme document with categories and definitions.

Prompt: As an Information Architect, develop a data classification scheme for a large enterprise. The goal is to ensure data security and compliance with regulations by categorizing various types of sensitive data. Please consider industry standards and privacy requirements. Provide a data classification scheme document with clear categories and definitions.

12.

[Role]: Information Architect
[Task]: Conduct a content gap analysis for a website redesign project.
[Context]: The analysis will compare existing and desired content.
[Goal]: Identify missing or outdated content and prioritize updates.
[Constraints]: Consider user needs and project timeline.
[Style or Tone]: Analytical, thorough, and actionable.
[Structure or Format]: Content gap analysis report with findings and recommendations.

Prompt: As an Information Architect, conduct a content gap analysis for a website redesign project. The goal is to identify missing or outdated content and prioritize updates by comparing existing and desired content. Please consider user needs and the project timeline. Provide a content gap analysis report with detailed findings and recommendations.

13.

[Role]: Information Architect
[Task]: Design an intuitive navigation menu for a mobile app.
[Context]: The app contains multiple features and sections.
[Goal]: Enable users to easily navigate and access content.
[Constraints]: Consider mobile screen limitations and user interactions.
[Style or Tone]: User-friendly, minimalistic, and visually appealing.
[Structure or Format]: Navigation menu design or prototype.

Prompt: As an Information Architect, design an intuitive navigation menu for a mobile app. The goal is to enable users to easily navigate and access content within the app, considering mobile screen limitations and user interactions. Provide a navigation menu design or prototype that is user-friendly, minimalistic, and visually appealing.

14.

[Role]: Information Architect
[Task]: Conduct a user needs analysis for a knowledge management system.
[Context]: The system will serve employees across departments.
[Goal]: Identify information requirements and user pain points.
[Constraints]: Use appropriate research methods and interviews.
[Style or Tone]: Empathetic, inquisitive, and evidence-based.
[Structure or Format]: User needs analysis report with insights and recommendations.

Prompt: As an Information Architect, conduct a user needs analysis for a knowledge management system. The goal is to identify information requirements and user pain points by using appropriate research methods and conducting interviews. Please approach the analysis with empathy, curiosity, and evidence-based insights. Provide a user needs analysis report with key insights and recommendations.

15.

[Role]: Information Architect
[Task]: Develop a content tagging system for a news publishing platform.
[Context]: The platform features articles from various topics and sources.
[Goal]: Enhance searchability and content discoverability.
[Constraints]: Consider user preferences and scalability.
[Style or Tone]: Consistent, descriptive, and user-oriented.
[Structure or Format]: Content tagging system framework or taxonomy.

Prompt: As an Information Architect, develop a content tagging system for a news publishing platform. The goal is to enhance searchability and content discoverability by creating a consistent, descriptive, and user-oriented tagging system. Please consider user preferences and scalability. Provide a content tagging system framework or taxonomy.

16.

[Role]: Information Architect
[Task]: Conduct a website performance analysis and optimization.
[Context]: The analysis will focus on loading speed and usability.
[Goal]: Improve website performance and user experience.
[Constraints]: Use appropriate performance analysis tools and techniques.
[Style or Tone]: Data-driven, diagnostic, and actionable.
[Structure or Format]: Website performance analysis report with recommendations.

Prompt: As an Information Architect, conduct a website performance analysis and optimization. The goal is to improve website performance and user experience by focusing on loading speed and usability. Please use appropriate performance analysis tools and techniques. Provide a website performance analysis report with detailed findings and recommendations.

17.

[Role]: Information Architect
[Task]: Create a content hierarchy for a government agency's website.
[Context]: The website contains a vast amount of information.
[Goal]: Organize content to improve findability and accessibility.
[Constraints]: Consider user needs and information categorization.
[Style or Tone]: Structured, logical, and user-centric.
[Structure or Format]: Content hierarchy diagram or visual representation.

Prompt: As an Information Architect, create a content hierarchy for a government agency's website. The goal is to organize content in a structured and logical manner to improve findability and accessibility. Please consider user needs and information categorization. Provide a content hierarchy diagram or visual representation.

18.

[Role]: Information Architect
[Task]: Conduct a usability testing session for a mobile banking app.
[Context]: The session will involve representative users and tasks.
[Goal]: Identify usability issues and gather user feedback.
[Constraints]: Use appropriate usability testing methods and metrics.
[Style or Tone]: Objective, observational, and user-focused.
[Structure or Format]: Usability testing report with findings and recommendations.

Prompt: As an Information Architect, conduct a usability testing session for a mobile banking app. The goal is to identify usability issues and gather user feedback by using appropriate usability testing methods and metrics. Please approach the session objectively, observe user interactions, and focus on user needs. Provide a usability testing report with detailed findings and recommendations.

19.

[Role]: Information Architect
[Task]: Develop a content migration plan for a website redesign project.
[Context]: The project involves transferring content to a new platform.
[Goal]: Ensure a smooth and seamless content transition.
[Constraints]: Consider content dependencies and technical requirements.
[Style or Tone]: Systematic, organized, and collaborative.
[Structure or Format]: Content migration plan document with steps and timelines.

Prompt: As an Information Architect, develop a content migration plan for a website redesign project. The goal is to ensure a smooth and seamless transition of content to a new platform. Please consider content dependencies and technical requirements. Provide a content migration plan document with clear steps and timelines.

20.
[Role]: Information Architect
[Task]: Conduct a competitive analysis of a company's digital presence.
[Context]: The analysis will compare the company's website and online platforms with competitors.
[Goal]: Identify strengths, weaknesses, and opportunities for improvement.
[Constraints]: Use appropriate research methods and tools.
[Style or Tone]: Comparative, critical, and actionable.
[Structure or Format]: Competitive analysis report with insights and recommendations.

Prompt: As an Information Architect, conduct a competitive analysis of a company's digital presence. The goal is to identify strengths, weaknesses, and opportunities for improvement by comparing the company's website and online platforms with competitors. Please use appropriate research methods and tools. Provide a competitive analysis report with detailed insights and recommendations.

21.
[Role]: Information Architect
[Task]: Design an information retrieval system for a digital library.
[Context]: The library contains a vast collection of diverse resources.
[Goal]: Enable users to efficiently search and access relevant information.
[Constraints]: Consider user search behavior and metadata organization.
[Style or Tone]: User-centric, efficient, and scalable.
[Structure or Format]: Information retrieval system prototype or wireframe.

Prompt: As an Information Architect, design an information retrieval system for a digital library. The goal is to enable users to efficiently search and access relevant information from a vast collection of diverse resources. Please consider user search behavior and metadata organization. Provide an information retrieval system prototype or wireframe that is user-centric, efficient, and scalable.

22.

[Role]: Information Architect
[Task]: Develop a taxonomy for a product categorization system.
[Context]: The system will be used for an e-commerce platform.
[Goal]: Enable effective product browsing and filtering.
[Constraints]: Consider industry standards and user mental models.
[Style or Tone]: Logical, intuitive, and comprehensive.
[Structure or Format]: Taxonomy framework or hierarchy.

Prompt: As an Information Architect, develop a taxonomy for a product categorization system in an e-commerce platform. The goal is to enable effective product browsing and filtering by creating a logical, intuitive, and comprehensive taxonomy. Please consider industry standards and user mental models. Provide a taxonomy framework or hierarchy.

23.

[Role]: Information Architect
[Task]: Conduct an information audit for a large-scale website.
[Context]: The audit will assess the quality and relevance of existing content.
[Goal]: Identify content gaps, redundancies, and opportunities.
[Constraints]: Use appropriate auditing methodologies and tools.
[Style or Tone]: Systematic, analytical, and actionable.
[Structure or Format]: Information audit report with findings and recommendations.

Prompt: As an Information Architect, conduct an information audit for a large-scale website. The goal is to identify content gaps, redundancies, and opportunities by assessing the quality and relevance of existing content. Please use appropriate auditing methodologies and tools. Provide an information audit report with detailed findings and recommendations.

24.

[Role]: Information Architect
[Task]: Design an effective information architecture for a knowledge base.
[Context]: The knowledge base will house various articles and resources.
[Goal]: Facilitate easy navigation and content discovery.
[Constraints]: Consider user information needs and scalability.
[Style or Tone]: Organized, intuitive, and user-friendly.
[Structure or Format]: Information architecture diagram or sitemap.

Prompt: As an Information Architect, design an effective information architecture for a knowledge base. The goal is to facilitate easy navigation and content discovery of various articles and resources. Please consider user information needs and scalability. Provide an information architecture diagram or sitemap that is organized, intuitive, and user-friendly.

25.

[Role]: Information Architect
[Task]: Design an intuitive and user-friendly site search experience.
[Context]: Enhancing the search functionality and usability of a website.
[Goal]: Improve search accuracy, speed, and relevance of results.
[Constraints]: Technical limitations and compatibility with existing systems.
[Style or Tone]: User-centered, clear, and responsive.
[Structure or Format]: Prepared search design prototypes and user interface guidelines.

Prompt: As an Information Architect, design an intuitive and user-friendly site search experience. The goal is to improve search accuracy, speed, and relevance of results. Please consider technical limitations and compatibility with existing systems, using a user-centered, clear, and responsive style. Provide prepared search design prototypes and user interface guidelines.

Prompts for UX Writers

1.

[Role]: UX Writer
[Task]: Create user-friendly microcopy for a mobile banking app's onboarding flow.
[Context]: The onboarding flow will guide users in setting up their accounts.
[Goal]: Communicate essential information clearly and concisely.
[Constraints]: Consider limited screen space and user comprehension.
[Style or Tone]: Friendly, informative, and conversational.
[Structure or Format]: Onboarding microcopy text for each step.

Prompt: As a UX Writer, create user-friendly microcopy for a mobile banking app's onboarding flow. The goal is to communicate essential information clearly and concisely to guide users in setting up their accounts. Please consider limited screen space and user comprehension. Provide onboarding microcopy text for each step that is friendly, informative, and conversational.

2.

[Role]: UX Writer
[Task]: Write error messages for a form validation on an e-commerce website.
[Context]: The error messages will appear when users submit invalid or incomplete information.
[Goal]: Help users understand and correct their form errors.
[Constraints]: Use clear and actionable language.
[Style or Tone]: Supportive, concise, and instructional.
[Structure or Format]: Error message text for each possible validation error.

Prompt: As a UX Writer, write error messages for a form validation on an e-commerce website. The goal is to help users understand and correct their form errors by providing clear and actionable error messages. Please use a supportive, concise, and instructional tone. Provide error message text for each possible validation error.

3.

[Role]: UX Writer
[Task]: Craft compelling product descriptions for an online marketplace.
[Context]: The descriptions will showcase the unique features and benefits of each product.
[Goal]: Influence user purchasing decisions and provide accurate information.
[Constraints]: Use persuasive language and avoid exaggeration.
[Style or Tone]: Engaging, informative, and trustworthy.
[Structure or Format]: Product description text for each listed item.

Prompt: As a UX Writer, craft compelling product descriptions for an online marketplace. The goal is to influence user purchasing decisions by showcasing the unique features and benefits of each product, while providing accurate information. Please use engaging, informative, and trustworthy language. Provide product description text for each listed item.

4.

[Role]: UX Writer
[Task]: Write clear and concise instructions for a productivity app's task management feature.
[Context]: The instructions will guide users in creating, organizing, and completing tasks.
[Goal]: Help users understand and effectively use the task management feature.
[Constraints]: Use simple language and provide step-by-step guidance.

[Style or Tone]: Direct, easy-to-follow, and action-oriented.
[Structure or Format]: Task management instructions for various actions.

Prompt: As a UX Writer, write clear and concise instructions for a productivity app's task management feature. The goal is to help users understand and effectively use the task management feature by providing direct, easy-to-follow, and action-oriented instructions. Please use simple language and provide step-by-step guidance. Provide task management instructions for various actions.

5.
[Role]: UX Writer
[Task]: Create engaging and informative tooltips for a travel booking website's search filters.
[Context]: The tooltips will appear when users hover over each filter option.
[Goal]: Clarify the purpose and functionality of the search filters.
[Constraints]: Keep tooltips brief and easily scannable.
[Style or Tone]: Informal, helpful, and descriptive.
[Structure or Format]: Tooltip text for each search filter option.

Prompt: As a UX Writer, create engaging and informative tooltips for a travel booking website's search filters. The goal is to clarify the purpose and functionality of the search filters by providing brief and easily scannable tooltips. Please use an informal, helpful, and descriptive tone. Provide tooltip text for each search filter option.

6.
[Role]: UX Writer
[Task]: Write persuasive and user-centric call-to-action (CTA) buttons for a subscription-based service.
[Context]: The CTAs will encourage users to sign up for the service.

[Goal]: Prompt users to take action and convert them into subscribers.
[Constraints]: Use compelling language and create a sense of urgency.
[Style or Tone]: Motivating, clear, and concise.
[Structure or Format]: CTA button text for different stages of the subscription process.

Prompt: As a UX Writer, write persuasive and user-centric call-to-action (CTA) buttons for a subscription-based service. The goal is to prompt users to take action and convert them into subscribers by using compelling language and creating a sense of urgency. Please use a motivating, clear, and concise tone. Provide CTA button text for different stages of the subscription process.

7.

[Role]: UX Writer
[Task]: Develop user-friendly and informative push notification messages for a food delivery app.
[Context]: The push notifications will provide updates on order status and special offers.
[Goal]: Engage users, provide relevant information, and encourage app usage.
[Constraints]: Keep messages concise and personalized.
[Style or Tone]: Friendly, time-sensitive, and enticing.
[Structure or Format]: Push notification message text for different scenarios.

Prompt: As a UX Writer, develop user-friendly and informative push notification messages for a food delivery app. The goal is to engage users, provide relevant information, and encourage app usage by using friendly, time-sensitive, and enticing messages. Please keep the messages concise and personalized. Provide push notification message text for different scenarios.

8.

[Role]: UX Writer
[Task]: Develop user onboarding content for a web application.
[Context]: Introducing new users to the features and functionality of the application.
[Goal]: Enhance user adoption and minimize user friction.
[Constraints]: Limited user attention and need for simplicity in explanations.
[Style or Tone]: Engaging, instructional, and encouraging.
[Structure or Format]: Prepared onboarding tutorial scripts and interactive tooltips.

Prompt: As a UX Writer, develop user onboarding content for a web application. The goal is to enhance user adoption and minimize user friction. Please consider the limited user attention and the need for simplicity in explanations, using an engaging, instructional, and encouraging style. Provide prepared onboarding tutorial scripts and interactive tooltips. chatbot response text for common customer queries.

9.

[Role]: UX Writer
[Task]: Create clear and concise error messages for a password reset form.
[Context]: The error messages will appear when users encounter issues during the password reset process.
[Goal]: Help users understand and resolve their password-related errors.
[Constraints]: Use plain language and provide actionable steps.
[Style or Tone]: Supportive, straightforward, and informative.
[Structure or Format]: Error message text for different password-related errors.

Prompt: As a UX Writer, create clear and concise error messages for a password reset form. The goal is to help users understand and resolve their password-related errors by using supportive, straightforward, and informative error messages. Please use plain language and provide actionable steps. Provide error message text for different password-related errors.

10.
[Role]: UX Writer
[Task]: Write informative and engaging product tour content for a software application.
[Context]: The product tour will introduce users to key features and functionalities.
[Goal]: Help users understand and navigate the software effectively.
[Constraints]: Use concise explanations and highlight key benefits.
[Style or Tone]: Informative, friendly, and interactive.
[Structure or Format]: Product tour content text for each step or feature.

Prompt: As a UX Writer, write informative and engaging product tour content for a software application. The goal is to help users understand and navigate the software effectively by using concise explanations and highlighting key benefits. Please use an informative, friendly, and interactive tone. Provide product tour content text for each step or feature.

11.
[Role]: UX Writer
[Task]: Craft user-friendly and persuasive onboarding emails for a mobile app.
[Context]: The emails will be sent to new users to guide them through the app's features.
[Goal]: Encourage user engagement and highlight key functionalities.
[Constraints]: Keep emails concise and action-oriented.
[Style or Tone]: Welcoming, informative, and enticing.
[Structure or Format]: Onboarding email content for different stages of user onboarding.

Prompt: As a UX Writer, craft user-friendly and persuasive onboarding emails for a mobile app. The goal is to encourage user engagement and highlight key functionalities by using welcoming, informative, and enticing content. Please keep the emails concise and action-oriented. Provide onboarding email content for different stages of user onboarding.

12.

[Role]: UX Writer
[Task]: Write informative and concise error messages for a multi-step checkout process.
[Context]: The error messages will appear when users encounter issues during the checkout.
[Goal]: Help users understand and resolve their checkout errors.
[Constraints]: Use clear language and provide troubleshooting suggestions.
[Style or Tone]: Supportive, informative, and problem-solving.
[Structure or Format]: Error message text for different checkout-related errors.

Prompt: As a UX Writer, write informative and concise error messages for a multi-step checkout process. The goal is to help users understand and resolve their checkout errors by using supportive, informative, and problem-solving error messages. Please use clear language and provide troubleshooting suggestions. Provide error message text for different checkout-related errors.

13.

[Role]: UX Writer
[Task]: Create engaging and informative in-app notifications for a social media platform.
[Context]: The notifications will inform users about new messages, mentions, and activities.
[Goal]: Prompt user engagement and encourage interaction.
[Constraints]: Keep notifications short and relevant.

[Style or Tone]: Personalized, attention-grabbing, and conversational.
[Structure or Format]: In-app notification text for different types of activities.

Prompt: As a UX Writer, create engaging and informative in-app notifications for a social media platform. The goal is to prompt user engagement and encourage interaction by using personalized, attention-grabbing, and conversational notifications. Please keep the notifications short and relevant. Provide in-app notification text for different types of activities.

14.
[Role]: UX Writer
[Task]: Write clear and concise in-product messaging for a software application's new feature.
[Context]: The messaging will inform users about the feature's availability and functionality.
[Goal]: Drive user adoption and provide guidance on using the new feature.
[Constraints]: Use straightforward language and highlight key benefits.
[Style or Tone]: Informative, accessible, and action-oriented.
[Structure or Format]: In-product messaging text for different touchpoints related to the new feature.

Prompt: As a UX Writer, write clear and concise in-product messaging for a software application's new feature. The goal is to drive user adoption and provide guidance on using the new feature by using informative, accessible, and action-oriented messaging. Please use straightforward language and highlight key benefits. Provide in-product messaging text for different touchpoints related to the new feature.

15.
[Role]: UX Writer
[Task]: Collaborate with the design team to create microcopy for interactive elements.

[Context]: Ensuring consistency and clarity in user interface text.
[Goal]: Enhance usability and guide users through interactions.
[Constraints]: Limited space for microcopy and adherence to brand voice.
[Style or Tone]: Concise, informative, and aligned with brand guidelines.
[Structure or Format]: Prepared microcopy guidelines and usage examples.

Prompt: As a UX Writer, collaborate with the design team to create microcopy for interactive elements. The goal is to enhance usability and guide users through interactions. Please consider the limited space for microcopy and adhere to the brand voice, using a concise, informative, and aligned style. Provide prepared microcopy guidelines and usage examples.

16.
[Role]: UX Writer
[Task]: Write informative and engaging tooltips for a web application's dashboard widgets.
[Context]: The tooltips will appear when users hover over each dashboard widget.
[Goal]: Clarify the purpose and functionality of the widgets.
[Constraints]: Keep tooltips concise and contextually relevant.
[Style or Tone]: Informative, concise, and visually appealing.
[Structure or Format]: Tooltip text for each dashboard widget.

Prompt: As a UX Writer, write informative and engaging tooltips for a web application's dashboard widgets. The goal is to clarify the purpose and functionality of the widgets by providing concise and contextually relevant tooltips. Please use an informative, concise, and visually appealing style. Provide tooltip text for each dashboard widget.

17.
[Role]: UX Writer
[Task]: Craft persuasive and user-centric landing page copy for a software product.

[Context]: The landing page will introduce the product and its key features.
[Goal]: Capture user interest and drive conversions.
[Constraints]: Use compelling language and highlight key benefits.
[Style or Tone]: Convincing, concise, and action-oriented.
[Structure or Format]: Landing page copy for different sections.

Prompt: As a UX Writer, craft persuasive and user-centric landing page copy for a software product. The goal is to capture user interest and drive conversions by using compelling language and highlighting key benefits. Please use a convincing, concise, and action-oriented tone. Provide landing page copy for different sections.

18.
[Role]: UX Writer
[Task]: Write clear and concise onboarding instructions for a mobile app's new feature.
[Context]: The instructions will guide users in using the feature for the first time.
[Goal]: Help users understand the feature's functionality and benefits.
[Constraints]: Use simple language and provide step-by-step guidance.
[Style or Tone]: Informative, friendly, and accessible.
[Structure or Format]: Onboarding instruction text for each step of using the feature.

Prompt: As a UX Writer, write clear and concise onboarding instructions for a mobile app's new feature. The goal is to help users understand the feature's functionality and benefits by using informative, friendly, and accessible instructions. Please use simple language and provide step-by-step guidance. Provide onboarding instruction text for each step of using the feature.

19.

[Role]: UX Writer
[Task]: Create user-friendly and informative FAQ content for a website.
[Context]: The FAQs will address common user queries and provide solutions.
[Goal]: Assist users in finding answers and resolving issues.
[Constraints]: Use clear language and provide comprehensive responses.
[Style or Tone]: Informative, concise, and easily scannable.
[Structure or Format]: FAQ content for different categories of questions.

Prompt: As a UX Writer, create user-friendly and informative FAQ content for a website. The goal is to assist users in finding answers and resolving issues by using informative, concise, and easily scannable content. Please use clear language and provide comprehensive responses. Provide FAQ content for different categories of questions.

20.

[Role]: UX Writer
[Task]: Write engaging and informative in-app notifications for a fitness tracking app.
[Context]: The notifications will provide updates on user progress and achievements.
[Goal]: Motivate users and keep them engaged with their fitness goals.
[Constraints]: Keep notifications concise and actionable.
[Style or Tone]: Encouraging, celebratory, and motivating.
[Structure or Format]: In-app notification text for different fitness milestones.

Prompt: As a UX Writer, write engaging and informative in-app notifications for a fitness tracking app. The goal is to motivate users and keep them engaged with their fitness goals by using encouraging, celebratory, and motivating notifications. Please keep the notifications concise and actionable. Provide in-app notification text for different fitness milestones.

21.
[Role]: UX Writer
[Task]: Create user-friendly and intuitive microcopy for a mobile app's onboarding screens.
[Context]: The microcopy will guide users through the onboarding process.
[Goal]: Provide clear instructions and highlight key app features.
[Constraints]: Keep the microcopy concise and easy to understand.
[Style or Tone]: Informative, friendly, and visually appealing.
[Structure or Format]: Microcopy text for each onboarding screen.

Prompt: As a UX Writer, create user-friendly and intuitive microcopy for a mobile app's onboarding screens. The goal is to provide clear instructions and highlight key app features by using informative, friendly, and visually appealing microcopy. Please keep the microcopy concise and easy to understand. Provide microcopy text for each onboarding screen.

22.
[Role]: UX Writer
[Task]: Write conversational and informative push notification messages for a news app.
[Context]: The push notifications will inform users about breaking news and updates.
[Goal]: Capture user attention and encourage them to read the full news articles.
[Constraints]: Keep the messages concise and engaging.
[Style or Tone]: Conversational, intriguing, and urgent.
[Structure or Format]: Push notification text for different news categories.

Prompt: As a UX Writer, write conversational and informative push notification messages for a news app. The goal is to capture user attention and encourage them to read the full news articles by using conversational, intriguing, and urgent messages. Please keep the messages concise and engaging. Provide push notification text for different news categories.

23.

[Role]: UX Writer
[Task]: Craft user-friendly and accessible error messages for a web form.
[Context]: The error messages will appear when users make mistakes while submitting the form.
[Goal]: Help users identify and correct their errors.
[Constraints]: Use clear and concise language, providing specific guidance.
[Style or Tone]: Supportive, informative, and actionable.
[Structure or Format]: Error message text for different types of form errors.

Prompt: As a UX Writer, craft user-friendly and accessible error messages for a web form. The goal is to help users identify and correct their errors by using supportive, informative, and actionable error messages. Please use clear and concise language, providing specific guidance. Provide error message text for different types of form errors.

24.

[Role]: UX Writer
[Task]: Write persuasive and compelling product descriptions for an e-commerce website.
[Context]: The product descriptions will showcase the features and benefits of each product.
[Goal]: Drive user interest and increase conversion rates.
[Constraints]: Use persuasive language and highlight unique selling points.
[Style or Tone]: Captivating, persuasive, and customer-centric.
[Structure or Format]: Product description text for different product categories.

Prompt: As a UX Writer, write persuasive and compelling product descriptions for an e-commerce website. The goal is to drive user interest and increase conversion rates by using captivating, persuasive, and customer-centric product descriptions. Please use persuasive language and highlight unique selling points. Provide product description text for different product categories.

25.

[Role]: UX Writer
[Task]: Create engaging and informative on-screen instructions for a mobile app's photo editing feature.
[Context]: The instructions will guide users in using the photo editing tools effectively.
[Goal]: Help users enhance their photos and achieve desired effects.
[Constraints]: Use step-by-step guidance and visual examples.
[Style or Tone]: Informative, friendly, and visually appealing.
[Structure or Format]: On-screen instruction text for each photo editing tool.

Prompt: Create engaging and informative on-screen instructions for a mobile app's photo editing feature. The instructions will guide users in using the photo editing tools effectively. Help users enhance their photos and achieve desired effects. Use step-by-step guidance and visual examples. Informative, friendly, and visually appealing., On-screen instruction text for each photo editing tool.

Prompts for Copywriters

1.

[Role]: Copywriter
[Task]: Develop attention-grabbing headlines for a marketing campaign.
[Context]: The headlines will be used in digital advertisements and social media posts.
[Goal]: Capture audience attention and generate interest in the product or service.
[Constraints]: Keep headlines concise and compelling.
[Style or Tone]: Creative, engaging, and impactful.
[Structure or Format]: Headline text for different marketing messages.

Prompt: As a Copywriter, develop attention-grabbing headlines for a marketing campaign. The goal is to capture audience attention and generate interest in the product or service by using creative, engaging, and impactful headlines. Please keep the headlines concise and compelling. Provide headline text for different marketing messages.

2.
[Role]: Copywriter
[Task]: Write persuasive and compelling email subject lines for a promotional campaign.
[Context]: The subject lines will be used to encourage email open rates and engagement.
[Goal]: Drive recipients to open and read the promotional emails.
[Constraints]: Keep subject lines concise and intriguing.
[Style or Tone]: Persuasive, curiosity-inducing, and enticing.
[Structure or Format]: Email subject line text for different promotional emails.

Prompt: As a Copywriter, write persuasive and compelling email subject lines for a promotional campaign. The goal is to drive recipients to open and read the promotional emails by using persuasive, curiosity-inducing, and enticing subject lines. Please keep the subject lines concise and intriguing. Provide email subject line text for different promotional emails.

3.
[Role]: Copywriter
[Task]: Craft engaging and informative product descriptions for an online marketplace.
[Context]: The product descriptions will appear on individual product pages.
[Goal]: Inform potential buyers about the product's features and benefits.
[Constraints]: Use descriptive language and highlight unique selling points.

[Style or Tone]: Informative, persuasive, and customer-centric.
[Structure or Format]: Product description text for different product listings.

Prompt: As a Copywriter, craft engaging and informative product descriptions for an online marketplace. The goal is to inform potential buyers about the product's features and benefits by using informative, persuasive, and customer-centric descriptions. Please use descriptive language and highlight unique selling points. Provide product description text for different product listings.

4.
[Role]: Copywriter
[Task]: Write compelling and persuasive ad copy for an online magazine.
[Context]: The ad copy will be used to promote a specific product or service.
[Goal]: Capture readers' attention and generate interest in the offering.
[Constraints]: Keep ad copy concise and visually impactful.
[Style or Tone]: Captivating, persuasive, and visually appealing.
[Structure or Format]: Ad copy text for different magazine ad placements.

Prompt: As a Copywriter, write compelling and persuasive ad copy for an online magazine. The goal is to capture readers' attention and generate interest in the offering by using captivating, persuasive, and visually appealing ad copy. Please keep the ad copy concise and visually impactful. Provide ad copy text for different magazine ad placements.

5.
[Role]: Copywriter
[Task]: Develop catchy and memorable slogans for a brand or product.
[Context]: The slogans will be used in advertising campaigns and brand messaging.
[Goal]: Create brand recognition and establish a strong brand identity.

[Constraints]: Keep slogans short, memorable, and reflective of the brand.
[Style or Tone]: Creative, catchy, and brand-aligned.
[Structure or Format]: Slogan text for different brand or product messages.

Prompt: As a Copywriter, develop catchy and memorable slogans for a brand or product. The goal is to create brand recognition and establish a strong brand identity by using creative, catchy, and brand-aligned slogans. Please keep the slogans short, memorable, and reflective of the brand. Provide slogan text for different brand or product messages.

6.
[Role]: Copywriter
[Task]: Create engaging email newsletters for a subscription service.
[Context]: Your role is to craft captivating newsletters that inform and retain subscribers of a subscription service.
[Goal]: Create compelling content that informs, entertains, and encourages continued engagement.
[Constraints]: Limited reader attention, personalized content based on preferences and behavior, brand consistency.
[Style or Tone]: Conversational, informative, personalized.
[Structure or Format]: Attention-grabbing subject lines, engaging openings, clear sections, relevant visuals.

Prompt: As a Copywriter, your task is writing engaging email newsletters. Craft subject lines that entice subscribers to open and explore. Start with captivating openings that grab attention and encourage reading. Organize into clear sections for easy navigation. Use relevant visuals to enhance appeal. Personalize content based on preferences and behavior, making each newsletter tailored. Your goal is to create valuable newsletters that keep subscribers engaged, contributing to retention and satisfaction.

7.
[Role]: Copywriter
[Task]: Craft copy for an in-person tech event.
[Context]: You are tasked with creating compelling and engaging copy for

an upcoming in-person tech event, targeting industry professionals and enthusiasts.
[Goal]: Generate excitement, communicate key event details, and encourage attendance and engagement.
[Constraints]: Limited space for copy, need to convey essential information concisely, aligning with the event's branding and tone.
[Style or Tone]: Energetic, informative, and persuasive.
[Structure or Format]: Headlines, taglines, event descriptions, social media posts, and email announcements.

Prompt: As a Copywriter, your expertise is crucial in generating buzz and driving attendance for the upcoming in-person tech event. Craft attention-grabbing headlines that capture the essence of the event and spark curiosity. Create concise event descriptions that highlight key features, such as guest speakers, workshops, and networking opportunities. Showcase the value and benefits attendees can expect, emphasizing the practical knowledge, industry insights, and networking connections they will gain. Develop engaging social media posts and email announcements that build anticipation and encourage registration. Leverage the event's branding guidelines to maintain consistency in messaging, ensuring it aligns with the event's tone and values. Your goal is to convey the event's unique value proposition, create excitement, and persuade the target audience to attend and actively participate.

8.

[Role]: Copywriter
[Task]: Create ad copy for a digital campaign.
[Context]: Craft persuasive copy to boost traffic, conversions, and sales.
[Goal]: Create attention-grabbing, compelling ad copy that compels action.
[Constraints]: Limited space, platform guidelines, target audience.
[Style or Tone]: Captivating, persuasive, action-oriented.
[Structure or Format]: Concise headlines, compelling text, clear call-to-action.

Prompt: As a Copywriter, create attention-grabbing ad copy. Craft headlines that capture attention and pique curiosity. Write persuasive copy highlighting benefits and value. Use action-oriented language and storytelling to drive action. Adhere to guidelines, resonate with the target audience. Stand out, capture interest, compel action. The goal is to drive traffic, conversions, and sales.

9.

[Role]: Copywriter
[Task]: Develop engaging blog articles on industry-related topics.
[Context]: Providing informative and entertaining content for the target audience.
[Goal]: Drive website traffic and establish thought leadership.
[Constraints]: Limited word count and SEO optimization.
[Style or Tone]: Informative, engaging, and conversational.
[Structure or Format]: Prepared blog article outline and content guidelines.

Prompt: As a Copywriter, develop engaging blog articles on industry-related topics. The goal is to drive website traffic and establish thought leadership. Please consider the limited word count and SEO optimization, using an informative, engaging, and conversational style. Provide a prepared blog article outline and content guidelines.

10.

[Role]: Copywriter
[Task]: Craft a compelling brand story for a startup company.
[Context]: Develop a captivating brand story that communicates values, mission, and unique identity.
[Goal]: Create a narrative that establishes an emotional connection.
[Constraints]: Limited word count, align with brand identity, differentiate from competitors.
[Style or Tone]: Authentic, inspiring, storytelling.
[Structure or Format]: Engaging opening, clear progression, memorable closing statement.

Prompt: As a Copywriter, create a brand story capturing the essence of the startup. Begin with an engaging opening, sparking curiosity instantly. Progress, highlighting values, mission, and unique identity. Use storytelling techniques to connect emotionally, sharing the company's journey and desired impact. Align the story with the brand's identity, differentiating it from competitors. Conclude with a memorable closing, leaving a lasting impression and reinforcing the brand's value proposition. Your goal is a brand story that evokes emotion and forges a strong connection between the brand and its customers.

11.

[Role]: Copywriter
[Task]: Create compelling blog post titles for a content marketing strategy.
[Context]: The blog post titles will be used to attract readers and increase website traffic.
[Goal]: Generate interest, encourage click-throughs, and drive engagement.
[Constraints]: Keep titles concise, informative, and SEO-friendly.
[Style or Tone]: Captivating, informative, and attention-grabbing.
[Structure or Format]: Blog post title text for different content topics.

Prompt: As a Copywriter, create compelling blog post titles for a content marketing strategy. The goal is to generate interest, encourage click-throughs, and drive engagement. Please keep the titles concise, informative, and SEO-friendly, using a captivating, informative, and attention-grabbing writing style. Provide blog post title text for different content topics.

12.

[Role]: Copywriter
[Task]: Develop persuasive scripts for radio advertisements.
[Context]: The scripts will be used for promoting products or services through radio channels.
[Goal]: Capture listeners' attention, convey the message effectively, and drive action.
[Constraints]: Keep scripts concise, memorable, and aligned with the target audience.

[Style or Tone]: Convincing, engaging, and impactful.
[Structure or Format]: Script text for different radio ad durations and themes.

Prompt: As a Copywriter, develop persuasive scripts for radio advertisements. The goal is to capture listeners' attention, convey the message effectively, and drive action. Please keep the scripts concise, memorable, and aligned with the target audience, using a convincing, engaging, and impactful writing style. Provide script text for different radio ad durations and themes.

13.
[Role]: Copywriter
[Task]: Write compelling video scripts for promotional videos.
[Context]: The video scripts will be used to showcase products or services on various platforms.
[Goal]: Engage viewers, highlight key features, and inspire action.
[Constraints]: Keep scripts concise, visually descriptive, and emotionally engaging.
[Style or Tone]: Persuasive, dynamic, and visually stimulating.
[Structure or Format]: Script text for different video durations and styles.

Prompt: As a Copywriter, write compelling video scripts for promotional videos. The goal is to engage viewers, highlight key features, and inspire action. Please keep the scripts concise, visually descriptive, and emotionally engaging, using a persuasive, dynamic, and visually stimulating writing style. Provide script text for different video durations and styles.

14.
[Role]: Copywriter
[Task]: Create persuasive call-to-action (CTA) statements for landing pages.
[Context]: The CTAs will be placed strategically to encourage conversions.
[Goal]: Motivate visitors to take the desired action (e.g., sign up, make a purchase).

[Constraints]: Keep CTAs concise, clear, and compelling.
[Style or Tone]: Action-oriented, persuasive, and urgency-driven.
[Structure or Format]: Call-to-action text for different landing page sections.

Prompt: As a Copywriter, create persuasive call-to-action (CTA) statements for landing pages. The goal is to motivate visitors to take the desired action (e.g., sign up, make a purchase) by using concise, clear, and compelling CTAs. Please adopt an action-oriented, persuasive, and urgency-driven writing style. Provide CTA text for different landing page sections.

15.

[Role]: Copywriter
[Task]: Develop engaging social media captions for a brand's Instagram posts.
[Context]: The captions will accompany visual content to captivate the target audience.
[Goal]: Increase reach, encourage interaction, and promote brand awareness.
[Constraints]: Keep captions concise, relevant, and aligned with the brand's voice.
[Style or Tone]: Conversational, relatable, and hashtag-friendly.
[Structure or Format]: Social media caption text for different Instagram posts.

Prompt: As a Copywriter, develop engaging social media captions for a brand's Instagram posts. The goal is to increase reach, encourage interaction, and promote brand awareness. Please keep the captions concise, relevant, and aligned with the brand's voice, using a conversational, relatable, and hashtag-friendly writing style. Provide social media caption text for different Instagram posts.

16.

[Role]: Copywriter
[Task]: Develop a brand voice and tone that authentically represents the brand's personality and values.
[Context]: Enhancing brand identity and establishing consistent communication across various channels.
[Goal]: Create a unique brand voice that resonates with the target audience and differentiates the brand from competitors.
[Constraints]: Adherence to brand guidelines, consideration of target audience demographics and preferences, aligning with industry-specific norms.
[Style or Tone]: Creative, adaptable, and aligned with the brand's personality.
[Structure or Format]: Create a brand voice guide that includes guidelines for developing a distinct brand voice and tone, examples of tone in different contexts, and strategies for maintaining consistency.

Prompt: As a Copywriter, one of your key tasks is to develop a brand voice and tone that authentically represents the brand's personality and values. Create a comprehensive brand voice guide that provides guidelines for crafting unique and consistent copy. Consider the brand's identity, target audience demographics, and preferences. Ensure adherence to brand guidelines while allowing room for creativity and adaptation. Your goal is to create a brand voice that resonates with the target audience and differentiates the brand from competitors. Include examples of tone in different contexts, such as marketing campaigns, social media posts, and customer support communications. Additionally, provide strategies for maintaining consistency in brand voice across various channels and touchpoints to create a cohesive and memorable brand experience.

17.

[Role]: Copywriter
[Task]: Craft compelling product taglines for a new product launch.

[Context]: The taglines will be used in marketing materials, packaging, and advertisements.
[Goal]: Create memorable and impactful statements that resonate with the target audience.
[Constraints]: Keep taglines concise, unique, and reflective of the product's key benefits.
[Style or Tone]: Catchy, persuasive, and brand-centric.
[Structure or Format]: Tagline text for different product messaging.

Prompt: As a Copywriter, craft compelling product taglines for a new product launch. The goal is to create memorable and impactful statements that resonate with the target audience. Please keep the taglines concise, unique, and reflective of the product's key benefits, using a catchy, persuasive, and brand-centric writing style. Provide tagline text for different product messaging.

18.
[Role]: Copywriter
[Task]: Write engaging website copy for a company's homepage.
[Context]: The copy will be used to introduce the company and its offerings to visitors.
[Goal]: Capture attention, communicate value proposition, and encourage further exploration.
[Constraints]: Keep copy informative, concise, and in line with the company's brand voice.
[Style or Tone]: Professional, compelling, and customer-focused.
[Structure or Format]: Website copy text for different sections of the homepage.

Prompt: As a Copywriter, write engaging website copy for a company's homepage. The goal is to capture attention, communicate the value proposition, and encourage further exploration. Please keep the copy informative, concise, and in line with the company's brand voice, using a professional, compelling, and customer-focused writing style. Provide website copy text for different sections of the homepage.

19.

[Role]: Copywriter
[Task]: Develop persuasive sales scripts for telemarketing calls.
[Context]: The scripts will be used by sales representatives to promote products or services.
[Goal]: Capture prospects' interest, convey benefits, and generate sales leads.
[Constraints]: Keep scripts conversational, persuasive, and focused on customer needs.
[Style or Tone]: Friendly, persuasive, and solution-oriented.
[Structure or Format]: Script text for different stages of the telemarketing call.

Prompt: As a Copywriter, develop persuasive sales scripts for telemarketing calls. The goal is to capture prospects' interest, convey the benefits, and generate sales leads. Please keep the scripts conversational, persuasive, and focused on customer needs, using a friendly, persuasive, and solution-oriented writing style. Provide script text for different stages of the telemarketing call.

20.

[Role]: Copywriter
[Task]: Write engaging and informative blog articles for a content marketing strategy.
[Context]: The articles will be published on the company's blog to educate and engage readers.
[Goal]: Provide valuable information, establish thought leadership, and drive website traffic.
[Constraints]: Keep articles well-researched, informative, and aligned with target audience interests.

[Style or Tone]: Informative, authoritative, and reader-friendly.
[Structure or Format]: Blog article text for different content topics.

Prompt: As a Copywriter, write engaging and informative blog articles for a content marketing strategy. The goal is to provide valuable information, establish thought leadership, and drive website traffic. Please keep the articles well-researched, informative, and aligned with the target audience's interests, using an informative, authoritative, and reader-friendly writing style. Provide blog article text for different content topics.

21.
[Role]: Copywriter
[Task]: Create persuasive sales brochures for a new product or service.
[Context]: The brochures will be used to provide information and entice potential customers.
[Goal]: Showcase product features, highlight benefits, and encourage conversion.
[Constraints]: Keep brochures visually appealing, concise, and aligned with the brand's style.
[Style or Tone]: Persuasive, visually descriptive, and brand-aligned.
[Structure or Format]: Brochure text for different sections and layouts.

Prompt: As a Copywriter, create persuasive sales brochures for a new product or service. The goal is to showcase product features, highlight benefits, and encourage conversion. Please keep the brochures visually appealing, concise, and aligned with the brand's style, using a persuasive, visually descriptive, and brand-aligned writing style. Provide brochure text for different sections and layouts.

22.
[Role]: Copywriter
[Task]: Develop engaging email marketing campaigns for a promotional offer.

[Context]: The emails will be sent to a targeted customer base to promote a limited-time offer.
[Goal]: Drive conversions, generate interest, and encourage recipients to take action.
[Constraints]: Keep emails concise, personalized, and aligned with the brand's messaging.
[Style or Tone]: Compelling, persuasive, and customer-centric.
[Structure or Format]: Email text for different stages of the campaign.

Prompt: As a Copywriter, develop engaging email marketing campaigns for a promotional offer. The goal is to drive conversions, generate interest, and encourage recipients to take action. Please keep the emails concise, personalized, and aligned with the brand's messaging, using a compelling, persuasive, and customer-centric writing style. Provide email text for different stages of the campaign.

23.
[Role]: Copywriter
[Task]: Craft compelling headlines and descriptions for online advertisements.
[Context]: The advertisements will be displayed on various platforms to attract clicks.
[Goal]: Capture attention, convey key messages, and drive click-through rates.
[Constraints]: Keep headlines and descriptions concise, impactful, and aligned with the ad's purpose.
[Style or Tone]: Attention-grabbing, persuasive, and action-oriented.
[Structure or Format]: Headline and description text for different ad formats.

Prompt: As a Copywriter, craft compelling headlines and descriptions for online advertisements. The goal is to capture attention, convey key messages, and drive click-through rates. Please keep the headlines and descriptions concise, impactful, and aligned with the ad's purpose, using attention-grabbing, persuasive, and action-oriented writing style. Provide headline and description text for different ad formats.

24.

[Role]: Copywriter
[Task]: Write engaging product descriptions for an e-commerce website.
[Context]: The descriptions will be displayed alongside products to inform and persuade shoppers.
[Goal]: Highlight product features, evoke desire, and drive sales.
[Constraints]: Keep descriptions concise, informative, and aligned with the brand's voice.
[Style or Tone]: Descriptive, enticing, and customer-focused.
[Structure or Format]: Product description text for different product categories.

Prompt: As a Copywriter, write engaging product descriptions for an e-commerce website. The goal is to highlight product features, evoke desire, and drive sales. Please keep the descriptions concise, informative, and aligned with the brand's voice, using a descriptive, enticing, and customer-focused writing style. Provide product description text for different product categories.

25.

[Role]: Copywriter
[Task]: Develop persuasive scripts for YouTube ads.
[Context]: The scripts will be used to promote products or services through YouTube advertising.
[Goal]: Capture viewers' attention, convey benefits, and generate brand recall.
[Constraints]: Keep scripts concise, impactful, and aligned with the target audience.
[Style or Tone]: Engaging, persuasive, and visually descriptive.
[Structure or Format]: Script text for different durations and themes.

Prompt: As a Copywriter, develop persuasive scripts for YouTube ads. The goal is to capture viewers' attention, convey benefits, and generate brand recall. Please keep the scripts concise, impactful, and aligned with the target audience, using an engaging, persuasive, and visually descriptive writing style. Provide script text for different durations and themes.

Prompts for UX Editors

1.

[Role]: UX Editor
[Task]: Review and edit user interface (UI) copy for a mobile application.
[Context]: The UI copy includes buttons, labels, tooltips, and error messages.
[Goal]: Ensure clarity, consistency, and user-friendliness in the app's text elements.
[Constraints]: Follow brand guidelines, maintain a consistent tone, and improve readability.
[Style or Tone]: Clear, concise, and user-centric.
[Structure or Format]: Edited UI copy for different screens and elements.

Prompt: As a UX Editor, review and edit user interface (UI) copy for a mobile application. The goal is to ensure clarity, consistency, and user-friendliness in the app's text elements. Please follow brand guidelines, maintain a consistent tone, and improve readability, using a clear, concise, and user-centric editing style. Provide edited UI copy for different screens and elements.

2.

[Role]: UX Editor
[Task]: Proofread and refine user documentation for a software product.
[Context]: The documentation includes user manuals, guides, and FAQs.
[Goal]: Ensure accuracy, clarity, and ease of understanding for end users.

[Constraints]: Follow documentation standards, eliminate jargon, and improve structure.
[Style or Tone]: Professional, accessible, and informative.
[Structure or Format]: Proofread and refined user documentation text for different sections.

Prompt: As a UX Editor, proofread and refine user documentation for a software product. The goal is to ensure accuracy, clarity, and ease of understanding for end users. Please follow documentation standards, eliminate jargon, and improve the structure, using a professional, accessible, and informative editing style. Provide proofread and refined user documentation text for different sections.

3.
[Role]: UX Editor
[Task]: Review and enhance the readability of long-form articles on a website.
[Context]: The articles are informative and aim to engage the target audience.
[Goal]: Improve readability, flow, and user engagement.
[Constraints]: Maintain the author's voice, enhance subheadings, and optimize paragraph structure.
[Style or Tone]: Engaging, clear, and well-structured.
[Structure or Format]: Edited long-form article text with improved readability.

Prompt: As a UX Editor, review and enhance the readability of long-form articles on a website. The goal is to improve readability, flow, and user engagement. Please maintain the author's voice, enhance subheadings, and optimize paragraph structure, using an engaging, clear, and well-structured editing style. Provide edited long-form article text with improved readability.

4.

[Role]: UX Editor
[Task]: Edit and refine microcopy for a mobile app's onboarding process.
[Context]: The microcopy includes tooltips, error messages, and success notifications.
[Goal]: Improve clarity, usability, and user satisfaction during onboarding.
[Constraints]: Maintain consistency, optimize button labels, and enhance instructional text.
[Style or Tone]: Friendly, concise, and action-oriented.
[Structure or Format]: Edited microcopy text for different onboarding steps.

Prompt: As a UX Editor, edit and refine microcopy for a mobile app's onboarding process. The goal is to improve clarity, usability, and user satisfaction during onboarding. Please maintain consistency, optimize button labels, and enhance instructional text, using a friendly, concise, and action-oriented editing style. Provide edited microcopy text for different onboarding steps.

5.

[Role]: UX Editor
[Task]: Review and revise error messages for a web application.
[Context]: The error messages provide feedback to users when an error occurs.
[Goal]: Enhance clarity, guidance, and user-friendliness in error communication.
[Constraints]: Keep messages concise, specific, and actionable.
[Style or Tone]: Clear, empathetic, and problem-solving.
[Structure or Format]: Revised error message text for different scenarios.

Prompt: As a UX Editor, review and revise error messages for a web application. The goal is to enhance clarity, guidance, and user-friendliness in error communication. Please keep the messages concise, specific, and actionable, using a clear, empathetic, and problem-solving editing style. Provide revised error message text for different scenarios.

6.

[Role]: UX Editor
[Task]: Proofread and edit user surveys to ensure accuracy and clarity.
[Context]: The surveys collect feedback from users to improve the user experience.
[Goal]: Enhance the quality of survey questions and response options.
[Constraints]: Maintain survey structure, adhere to research objectives, and improve readability.
[Style or Tone]: Professional, neutral, and unbiased.
[Structure or Format]: Proofread and edited user survey questions and response options.

Prompt: As a UX Editor, proofread and edit user surveys to ensure accuracy and clarity. The goal is to enhance the quality of survey questions and response options. Please maintain the survey structure, adhere to research objectives, and improve readability, using a professional, neutral, and unbiased editing style. Provide proofread and edited user survey questions and response options.

7.

[Role]: UX Editor
[Task]: Review and refine in-app notifications for a mobile application.
[Context]: The notifications provide important updates and prompts to users.
[Goal]: Improve clarity, relevance, and user interaction with notifications.
[Constraints]: Maintain the app's tone and style, optimize call-to-action text, and reduce redundancy.
[Style or Tone]: Concise, informative, and action-oriented.
[Structure or Format]: Refined in-app notification text for different scenarios.

Prompt: As a UX Editor, review and refine in-app notifications for a mobile application. The goal is to improve clarity, relevance, and user interaction with notifications. Please maintain the app's tone and style, optimize call-to-action text, and reduce redundancy, using a concise, informative, and action-oriented editing style. Provide refined in-app notification text for different scenarios.

8.

[Role]: UX Editor
[Task]: Edit and enhance the conversational flow of a chatbot's responses.
[Context]: The chatbot engages with users and provides information or assistance.
[Goal]: Improve the naturalness, clarity, and helpfulness of the chatbot's dialogue.
[Constraints]: Maintain the chatbot's purpose, optimize response length, and enhance contextual understanding.
[Style or Tone]: Conversational, friendly, and helpful.
[Structure or Format]: Edited chatbot response text for different user inquiries.

Prompt: As a UX Editor, edit and enhance the conversational flow of a chatbot's responses. The goal is to improve the naturalness, clarity, and helpfulness of the chatbot's dialogue. Please maintain the chatbot's purpose, optimize response length, and enhance contextual understanding, using a conversational, friendly, and helpful editing style. Provide edited chatbot response text for different user inquiries.

9.

[Role]: UX Editor
[Task]: Proofread and refine user interface (UI) labels for a web application.
[Context]: The labels are text elements that guide users in navigating the application.
[Goal]: Ensure consistency, clarity, and user-friendliness in UI labels.

[Constraints]: Follow UI design guidelines, improve label alignment, and enhance wording.
[Style or Tone]: Clear, concise, and intuitive.
[Structure or Format]: Proofread and refined UI label text for different interface components.

Prompt: As a UX Editor, proofread and refine user interface (UI) labels for a web application. The goal is to ensure consistency, clarity, and user-friendliness in UI labels. Please follow UI design guidelines, improve label alignment, and enhance wording, using a clear, concise, and intuitive editing style. Provide proofread and refined UI label text for different interface components.

10.
[Role]: UX Editor
[Task]: Review and revise user onboarding tutorials for a mobile app.
[Context]: The tutorials guide new users through the app's features and functionality.
[Goal]: Improve the clarity, comprehensibility, and effectiveness of the tutorials.
[Constraints]: Maintain the app's visual style, optimize step-by-step instructions, and enhance visual aids.
[Style or Tone]: Step-by-step, instructive, and user-friendly.
[Structure or Format]: Revised user onboarding tutorial text for different app features.

Prompt: As a UX Editor, review and revise user onboarding tutorials for a mobile app. The goal is to improve the clarity, comprehensibility, and effectiveness of the tutorials. Please maintain the app's visual style, optimize step-by-step instructions, and enhance visual aids, using a step-by-step, instructive, and user-friendly editing style. Provide revised user onboarding tutorial text for different app features.

11.

[Role]: UX Editor
[Task]: Edit and enhance the readability of a website's navigation menu.
[Context]: The navigation menu helps users navigate different sections of the website.
[Goal]: Improve clarity, ease of use, and findability of website sections.
[Constraints]: Maintain menu structure, optimize label length, and improve visual hierarchy.
[Style or Tone]: Clear, concise, and intuitive.
[Structure or Format]: Edited navigation menu text for different website sections.

Prompt: As a UX Editor, edit and enhance the readability of a website's navigation menu. The goal is to improve clarity, ease of use, and findability of website sections. Please maintain the menu structure, optimize label length, and improve visual hierarchy, using a clear, concise, and intuitive editing style. Provide edited navigation menu text for different website sections.

12.

[Role]: UX Editor
[Task]: Review and refine tooltips for a mobile app's interface elements.
[Context]: The tooltips provide additional information or guidance to users.
[Goal]: Enhance clarity, relevance, and discoverability of tooltips.
[Constraints]: Maintain consistency, optimize tooltip length, and improve visual styling.
[Style or Tone]: Informative, concise, and visually appealing.
[Structure or Format]: Refined tooltip text for different interface elements.

Prompt: As a UX Editor, review and refine tooltips for a mobile app's interface elements. The goal is to enhance clarity, relevance, and discoverability of tooltips. Please maintain consistency, optimize tooltip length, and improve visual styling, using an informative, concise, and visually appealing editing style. Provide refined tooltip text for different interface elements.

13.

[Role]: UX Editor
[Task]: Proofread and edit user-generated content on a community forum.
[Context]: The forum allows users to interact, ask questions, and share knowledge.
[Goal]: Ensure accuracy, readability, and adherence to community guidelines.
[Constraints]: Maintain user's voice, improve grammar and spelling, and enforce guidelines.
[Style or Tone]: Respectful, inclusive, and informative.
[Structure or Format]: Proofread and edited user-generated content for different forum threads.

Prompt: As a UX Editor, proofread and edit user-generated content on a community forum. The goal is to ensure accuracy, readability, and adherence to community guidelines. Please maintain the user's voice, improve grammar and spelling, and enforce guidelines, using a respectful, inclusive, and informative editing style. Provide proofread and edited user-generated content for different forum threads.

14.

[Role]: UX Editor
[Task]: Review and refine the tone of error messages in a mobile app.
[Context]: The error messages provide feedback to users when an error occurs.
[Goal]: Enhance clarity, empathy, and user-friendliness in error communication.
[Constraints]: Maintain error severity, optimize message length, and improve user guidance.

[Style or Tone]: Empathetic, concise, and helpful.
[Structure or Format]: Refined error message text for different error scenarios.

Prompt: As a UX Editor, review and refine the tone of error messages in a mobile app. The goal is to enhance clarity, empathy, and user-friendliness in error communication. Please maintain the error severity, optimize message length, and improve user guidance, using an empathetic, concise, and helpful editing style. Provide refined error message text for different error scenarios.

15.

[Role]: UX Editor
[Task]: Edit and improve the readability of a user research report.
[Context]: The report summarizes findings from user research studies.
[Goal]: Ensure clarity, coherence, and actionable insights in the report.
[Constraints]: Maintain research structure, optimize sentence structure, and improve data visualization.
[Style or Tone]: Objective, informative, and well-structured.
[Structure or Format]: Edited user research report text for different research findings.

Prompt: As a UX Editor, edit and improve the readability of a user research report. The goal is to ensure clarity, coherence, and actionable insights in the report. Please maintain the research structure, optimize sentence structure, and improve data visualization, using an objective, informative, and well-structured editing style. Provide edited user research report text for different research findings.

16.

[Role]: UX Editor
[Task]: Review and enhance the tone of customer support emails.
[Context]: The emails provide assistance and resolve user inquiries or issues.

[Goal]: Improve clarity, empathy, and customer satisfaction in email communication.
[Constraints]: Maintain resolution steps, optimize email length, and improve response time.
[Style or Tone]: Polite, helpful, and professional.
[Structure or Format]: Enhanced customer support email text for different scenarios.

Prompt: As a UX Editor, review and enhance the tone of customer support emails. The goal is to improve clarity, empathy, and customer satisfaction in email communication. Please maintain the resolution steps, optimize email length, and improve response time, using a polite, helpful, and professional editing style. Provide enhanced customer support email text for different scenarios.

17.
[Role]: UX Editor
[Task]: Edit and refine the wording of call-to-action buttons on a website.
[Context]: The buttons encourage users to take specific actions or navigate to important sections.
[Goal]: Enhance clarity, persuasive impact, and usability of call-to-action buttons.
[Constraints]: Maintain visual consistency, optimize button text length, and improve visual prominence.
[Style or Tone]: Clear, compelling, and action-oriented.
[Structure or Format]: Edited call-to-action button text for different website sections.

Prompt: As a UX Editor, edit and refine the wording of call-to-action buttons on a website. The goal is to enhance clarity, persuasive impact, and usability of call-to-action buttons. Please maintain visual consistency, optimize button text length, and improve visual prominence, using a clear, compelling, and action-oriented editing style. Provide edited call-to-action button text for different website sections.

18.

[Role]: UX Editor

[Task]: Proofread and edit user interface (UI) notifications for a software application.

[Context]: The notifications inform users about important system events or updates.

[Goal]: Ensure accuracy, clarity, and user-friendliness in UI notifications.

[Constraints]: Maintain notification context, optimize notification length, and improve visual hierarchy.

[Style or Tone]: Informative, concise, and visually distinct.

[Structure or Format]: Proofread and edited UI notification text for different system events.

Prompt: As a UX Editor, proofread and edit user interface (UI) notifications for a software application. The goal is to ensure accuracy, clarity, and user-friendliness in UI notifications. Please maintain the notification context, optimize notification length, and improve visual hierarchy, using an informative, concise, and visually distinct editing style. Provide proofread and edited UI notification text for different system events.

19.

[Role]: UX Editor

[Task]: Review and refine the wording of tooltips in a web-based form.

[Context]: The tooltips provide additional information or guidance for form fields.

[Goal]: Improve clarity, relevance, and usability of tooltips.

[Constraints]: Maintain tooltip alignment, optimize tooltip length, and improve visual consistency.

[Style or Tone]: Clear, concise, and informative.

[Structure or Format]: Refined tooltip text for different form fields.

Prompt: As a UX Editor, review and refine the wording of tooltips in a web-based form. The goal is to improve clarity, relevance, and usability of tooltips. Please maintain tooltip alignment, optimize tooltip length, and improve visual consistency, using a clear, concise, and informative editing style. Provide refined tooltip text for different form fields.

20.

[Role]: UX Editor
[Task]: Edit and enhance the content of an instructional video script for a product.
[Context]: The video provides step-by-step guidance on using the product's features.
[Goal]: Ensure clarity, comprehensibility, and user engagement in the instructional video.
[Constraints]: Maintain video structure, optimize script length, and improve visual aids.
[Style or Tone]: Engaging, informative, and well-paced.
[Structure or Format]: Edited instructional video script for different product features.

Prompt: As a UX Editor, edit and enhance the content of an instructional video script for a product. The goal is to ensure clarity, comprehensibility, and user engagement in the instructional video. Please maintain the video structure, optimize script length, and improve visual aids, using an engaging, informative, and well-paced editing style. Provide edited instructional video script for different product features.

21.

[Role]: UX Editor
[Task]: Review and improve the readability of error messages in a mobile app.
[Context]: The error messages communicate issues or problems to users.
[Goal]: Enhance clarity, user-friendliness, and error resolution.

[Constraints]: Maintain error severity, optimize message length, and improve error handling instructions.
[Style or Tone]: Clear, concise, and helpful.
[Structure or Format]: Revised error message text for different error scenarios.

Prompt: As a UX Editor, review and improve the readability of error messages in a mobile app. The goal is to enhance clarity, user-friendliness, and error resolution. Please maintain the error severity, optimize message length, and improve error handling instructions, using a clear, concise, and helpful editing style. Provide revised error message text for different error scenarios.

22.
[Role]: UX Editor
[Task]: Edit and enhance the content of a user manual for a software product.
[Context]: The user manual provides instructions on using the software's features.
[Goal]: Ensure clarity, comprehensibility, and ease of use in the user manual.
[Constraints]: Maintain manual structure, optimize sentence structure, and improve visual aids.
[Style or Tone]: Informative, organized, and user-centric.
[Structure or Format]: Edited user manual text for different software features.

Prompt: As a UX Editor, edit and enhance the content of a user manual for a software product. The goal is to ensure clarity, comprehensibility, and ease of use in the user manual. Please maintain the manual structure, optimize sentence structure, and improve visual aids, using an informative, organized, and user-centric editing style. Provide edited user manual text for different software features.

23.
[Role]: UX Editor
[Task]: Proofread and edit the text of an in-app survey for a website.
[Context]: The survey collects user feedback and opinions about the website.
[Goal]: Ensure clarity, coherence, and ease of response in the survey.
[Constraints]: Maintain survey structure, optimize question length, and improve response options.
[Style or Tone]: Neutral, concise, and unbiased.
[Structure or Format]: Proofread and edited survey text for different survey questions.

Prompt: As a UX Editor, proofread and edit the text of an in-app survey for a website. The goal is to ensure clarity, coherence, and ease of response in the survey. Please maintain the survey structure, optimize question length, and improve response options, using a neutral, concise, and unbiased editing style. Provide proofread and edited survey text for different survey questions.

24.
[Role]: UX Editor
[Task]: Review and refine the wording of form field labels in a web application.
[Context]: The form fields collect user input or information.
[Goal]: Improve clarity, intuitiveness, and usability of form field labels.
[Constraints]: Maintain form structure, optimize label length, and improve visual alignment.
[Style or Tone]: Clear, descriptive, and user-friendly.
[Structure or Format]: Refined form field label text for different form sections.

Prompt: As a UX Editor, review and refine the wording of form field labels in a web application. The goal is to improve clarity, intuitiveness, and usability of form field labels. Please maintain the form structure, optimize label length, and improve visual alignment, using a clear, descriptive, and user-friendly editing style. Provide refined form field label text for different form sections.

25.

[Role]: UX Editor
[Task]: Edit and enhance the content of a knowledge base article for a software product.
[Context]: The knowledge base article provides instructions, tips, or troubleshooting guidance.
[Goal]: Ensure clarity, comprehensibility, and effectiveness of the knowledge base article.
[Constraints]: Maintain article structure, optimize sentence structure, and improve visual aids.
[Style or Tone]: Informative, concise, and user-centric.
[Structure or Format]: Edited knowledge base article text for different topics or sections.

Prompt: As a UX Editor, edit and enhance the content of a knowledge base article for a software product. The goal is to ensure clarity, comprehensibility, and effectiveness of the knowledge base article. Please maintain the article structure, optimize sentence structure, and improve visual aids, using an informative, concise, and user-centric editing style. Provide edited knowledge base article text for different topics or sections.

Prompts for Conversational Designers

1.

[Role]: Conversational Designer
[Task]: Design engaging and user-friendly chatbot interactions for a customer support scenario.
[Context]: The chatbot assists users with inquiries, troubleshooting, and issue resolution.
[Goal]: Improve chatbot's ability to provide accurate, helpful, and personalized responses.
[Constraints]: Maintain chatbot flow, optimize response length, and enhance natural language understanding.
[Style or Tone]: Friendly, conversational, and empathetic.
[Structure or Format]: Designed chatbot interaction flow for different customer support scenarios.

Prompt: As a Conversational Designer, design engaging and user-friendly chatbot interactions for a customer support scenario. The goal is to improve the chatbot's ability to provide accurate, helpful, and personalized responses. Please maintain the chatbot flow, optimize response length, and enhance natural language understanding, using a friendly, conversational, and empathetic design style. Provide designed chatbot interaction flow for different customer support scenarios.

2.

[Role]: Conversational Designer
[Task]: Create a conversational design for a virtual assistant helping users with travel planning.
[Context]: The virtual assistant assists users in booking flights, finding accommodations, and suggesting attractions.
[Goal]: Enhance virtual assistant's ability to provide personalized and helpful travel recommendations.

[Constraints]: Maintain virtual assistant's persona, optimize response length, and improve decision-making capabilities.
[Style or Tone]: Informative, helpful, and conversational.
[Structure or Format]: Created conversational design for different travel planning scenarios.

Prompt: As a Conversational Designer, create a conversational design for a virtual assistant helping users with travel planning. The goal is to enhance the virtual assistant's ability to provide personalized and helpful travel recommendations. Please maintain the virtual assistant's persona, optimize response length, and improve decision-making capabilities, using an informative, helpful, and conversational design style. Provide created conversational design for different travel planning scenarios.

3.
[Role]: Conversational Designer
[Task]: Design natural language interactions for a voice-controlled smart home assistant.
[Context]: The smart home assistant controls various devices, such as lights, thermostat, and entertainment systems.
[Goal]: Improve user experience by enabling intuitive and seamless voice commands and responses.
[Constraints]: Maintain smart home assistant's capabilities, optimize response length, and improve speech recognition accuracy.
[Style or Tone]: Clear, concise, and friendly.
[Structure or Format]: Designed natural language interactions for different smart home control scenarios.

Prompt: As a Conversational Designer, design natural language interactions for a voice-controlled smart home assistant. The goal is to improve the user experience by enabling intuitive and seamless voice commands and responses. Please maintain the smart home assistant's capabilities, optimize response length, and improve speech recognition accuracy, using a clear, concise, and friendly design style. Provide designed natural language interactions for different smart home control scenarios.

4.

[Role]: Conversational Designer
[Task]: Develop a conversational design for a virtual agent guiding users through an online shopping experience.
[Context]: The virtual agent helps users browse products, compare options, and make purchases.
[Goal]: Enhance virtual agent's ability to provide personalized product recommendations and shopping assistance.
[Constraints]: Maintain virtual agent's personality, optimize response length, and improve natural language understanding.
[Style or Tone]: Informative, persuasive, and customer-centric.
[Structure or Format]: Developed conversational design for different online shopping scenarios.

Prompt: As a Conversational Designer, develop a conversational design for a virtual agent guiding users through an online shopping experience. The goal is to enhance the virtual agent's ability to provide personalized product recommendations and shopping assistance. Please maintain the virtual agent's personality, optimize response length, and improve natural language understanding, using an informative, persuasive, and customer-centric design style. Provide developed conversational design for different online shopping scenarios.

5.

[Role]: Conversational Designer
[Task]: Create a conversational design for a language learning chatbot assisting users in practicing conversation skills.
[Context]: The chatbot provides language prompts, corrects pronunciation,

and offers vocabulary suggestions.
[Goal]: Improve chatbot's ability to provide engaging and effective language learning interactions.
[Constraints]: Maintain chatbot's pedagogical approach, optimize response length, and enhance error correction mechanisms.
[Style or Tone]: Supportive, encouraging, and educational.
[Structure or Format]: Created conversational design for different language learning exercises.

Prompt: As a Conversational Designer, create a conversational design for a language learning chatbot assisting users in practicing conversation skills. The goal is to improve the chatbot's ability to provide engaging and effective language learning interactions. Please maintain the chatbot's pedagogical approach, optimize response length, and enhance error correction mechanisms, using a supportive, encouraging, and educational design style. Provide created conversational design for different language learning exercises.

6.
[Role]: Conversational Designer
[Task]: Design conversational interactions for a virtual tour guide chatbot.
[Context]: The chatbot provides information, recommendations, and historical facts about tourist attractions.
[Goal]: Enhance the chatbot's ability to engage users and provide valuable insights during virtual tours.
[Constraints]: Maintain chatbot's knowledge base, optimize response length, and improve natural language understanding.
[Style or Tone]: Informative, engaging, and interactive.
[Structure or Format]: Designed conversational interactions for different tourist attractions.

Prompt: As a Conversational Designer, design conversational interactions for a virtual tour guide chatbot. The goal is to enhance the chatbot's ability to engage users and provide valuable insights during virtual tours. Please maintain the chatbot's knowledge base, optimize response length, and improve natural language understanding, using an informative, engaging, and interactive design style. Provide designed conversational interactions for different tourist attractions.

7.

[Role]: Conversational Designer
[Task]: Develop a conversational design for a healthcare chatbot assisting users with symptom analysis.
[Context]: The chatbot helps users assess symptoms, provides basic medical information, and recommends next steps.
[Goal]: Improve the chatbot's accuracy, empathy, and ability to guide users towards appropriate healthcare resources.
[Constraints]: Maintain chatbot's medical knowledge, optimize response length, and enhance user privacy and data security.
[Style or Tone]: Empathetic, informative, and supportive.
[Structure or Format]: Developed conversational design for different symptom analysis scenarios.

Prompt: As a Conversational Designer, develop a conversational design for a healthcare chatbot assisting users with symptom analysis. The goal is to improve the chatbot's accuracy, empathy, and ability to guide users towards appropriate healthcare resources. Please maintain the chatbot's medical knowledge, optimize response length, and enhance user privacy and data security, using an empathetic, informative, and supportive design style. Provide developed conversational design for different symptom analysis scenarios.

8.

[Role]: Conversational Designer
[Task]: Create conversational interactions for a food delivery chatbot taking users' orders.

[Context]: The chatbot allows users to browse menus, customize orders, and track delivery status.
[Goal]: Enhance the chatbot's usability, efficiency, and ability to handle complex order requests.
[Constraints]: Maintain chatbot's integration with ordering system, optimize response length, and improve order accuracy.
[Style or Tone]: Friendly, efficient, and customer-oriented.
[Structure or Format]: Created conversational interactions for different food ordering scenarios.

Prompt: As a Conversational Designer, create conversational interactions for a food delivery chatbot taking users' orders. The goal is to enhance the chatbot's usability, efficiency, and ability to handle complex order requests. Please maintain the chatbot's integration with the ordering system, optimize response length, and improve order accuracy, using a friendly, efficient, and customer-oriented design style. Provide created conversational interactions for different food ordering scenarios.

9.
[Role]: Conversational Designer
[Task]: Design conversational interactions for a virtual fitness coach chatbot.
[Context]: The chatbot provides exercise routines, tracks progress, and offers fitness advice.
[Goal]: Improve the chatbot's ability to motivate and guide users towards their fitness goals.
[Constraints]: Maintain chatbot's fitness knowledge, optimize response length, and enhance user feedback mechanisms.
[Style or Tone]: Motivational, informative, and supportive.
[Structure or Format]: Designed conversational interactions for different fitness activities.

Prompt: As a Conversational Designer, design conversational interactions for a virtual fitness coach chatbot. The goal is to improve the chatbot's ability to motivate and guide users towards their fitness goals. Please maintain the chatbot's fitness knowledge, optimize response length, and enhance user feedback mechanisms, using a motivational, informative, and supportive design style. Provide designed conversational interactions for different fitness activities.

10.

[Role]: Conversational Designer
[Task]: Develop a conversational design for a financial planning chatbot helping users with budgeting and saving.
[Context]: The chatbot provides personalized financial advice, tracks expenses, and suggests saving strategies.
[Goal]: Enhance the chatbot's ability to assist users in achieving their financial goals.
[Constraints]: Maintain chatbot's financial knowledge, optimize response length, and improve user data privacy.
[Style or Tone]: Informative, goal-oriented, and trustworthy.
[Structure or Format]: Developed conversational design for different financial planning scenarios.

Prompt: As a Conversational Designer, develop a conversational design for a financial planning chatbot helping users with budgeting and saving. The goal is to enhance the chatbot's ability to assist users in achieving their financial goals. Please maintain the chatbot's financial knowledge, optimize response length, and improve user data privacy, using an informative, goal-oriented, and trustworthy design style. Provide developed conversational design for different financial planning scenarios.

11.

[Role]: Conversational Designer

[Task]: Design conversational interactions for a mental health support chatbot.

[Context]: The chatbot provides emotional support, coping strategies, and resources for mental well-being.

[Goal]: Enhance the chatbot's ability to provide empathetic and effective support to users.

[Constraints]: Maintain chatbot's knowledge base, optimize response length, and ensure user privacy and confidentiality.

[Style or Tone]: Empathetic, compassionate, and non-judgmental.

[Structure or Format]: Designed conversational interactions for different mental health scenarios.

Prompt: As a Conversational Designer, design conversational interactions for a mental health support chatbot. The goal is to enhance the chatbot's ability to provide empathetic and effective support to users. Please maintain the chatbot's knowledge base, optimize response length, and ensure user privacy and confidentiality, using an empathetic, compassionate, and non-judgmental design style. Provide designed conversational interactions for different mental health scenarios.

12.

[Role]: Conversational Designer

[Task]: Develop a conversational and engaging chatbot script for a customer support chatbot.

[Context]: The chatbot will assist users with common inquiries and provide helpful solutions.

[Goal]: Create a seamless and personalized conversation flow.

[Constraints]: Consider different user scenarios and the limitations of the chatbot system.

[Style or Tone]: Natural, helpful, and contextually appropriate.

[Structure or Format]: Dialogue flows showcasing different user interactions.

Prompt: As a Content Designer, develop a conversational and engaging chatbot script for a customer support chatbot. The goal is to create a seamless and personalized conversation flow. Please consider different user scenarios and the limitations of the chatbot system. Provide dialogue flows showcasing different user interactions.

13.

[Role]: Conversational Designer
[Task]: Design conversational interactions for a personalized nutrition assistant chatbot.
[Context]: The chatbot provides dietary recommendations, tracks food intake, and offers healthy recipes.
[Goal]: Enhance the chatbot's ability to guide users towards healthier eating habits.
[Constraints]: Maintain chatbot's nutrition knowledge, optimize response length, and accommodate dietary restrictions.
[Style or Tone]: Informative, supportive, and non-judgmental.
[Structure or Format]: Designed conversational interactions for different nutritional scenarios.

Prompt: As a Conversational Designer, design conversational interactions for a personalized nutrition assistant chatbot. The goal is to enhance the chatbot's ability to guide users towards healthier eating habits. Please maintain the chatbot's nutrition knowledge, optimize response length, and accommodate dietary restrictions, using an informative, supportive, and non-judgmental design style. Provide designed conversational interactions for different nutritional scenarios.

14.

[Role]: Conversational Designer
[Task]: Develop a conversational design for a virtual mentor chatbot providing career guidance.

[Context]: The chatbot offers advice, career resources, and helps users explore job opportunities.
[Goal]: Improve the chatbot's ability to provide tailored career advice and support.
[Constraints]: Maintain chatbot's industry knowledge, optimize response length, and enhance user engagement.
[Style or Tone]: Informative, encouraging, and professional.
[Structure or Format]: Developed conversational design for different career guidance scenarios.

Prompt: As a Conversational Designer, develop a conversational design for a virtual mentor chatbot providing career guidance. The goal is to improve the chatbot's ability to provide tailored career advice and support. Please maintain the chatbot's industry knowledge, optimize response length, and enhance user engagement, using an informative, encouraging, and professional design style. Provide developed conversational design for different career guidance scenarios.

15.

[Role]: Conversational Designer
[Task]: Create conversational interactions for a travel planning chatbot assisting users with itinerary suggestions.
[Context]: The chatbot offers destination recommendations, travel tips, and helps users plan their trips.
[Goal]: Enhance the chatbot's ability to provide personalized and relevant travel recommendations.
[Constraints]: Maintain chatbot's travel knowledge, optimize response length, and consider user preferences.
[Style or Tone]: Informative, friendly, and inspiring.
[Structure or Format]: Created conversational interactions for different travel planning scenarios.

Prompt: As a Conversational Designer, create conversational interactions for a travel planning chatbot assisting users with itinerary suggestions. The goal is to enhance the chatbot's ability to provide personalized and relevant travel recommendations. Please maintain the chatbot's travel knowledge, optimize response length, and consider user preferences, using an informative, friendly, and inspiring design style. Provide created conversational interactions for different travel planning scenarios.

16.

[Role]: Conversational Designer

[Task]: Design conversational interactions for a customer support chatbot in the e-commerce industry.

[Context]: The chatbot handles inquiries, resolves issues, and provides product recommendations.

[Goal]: Improve the chatbot's efficiency and customer satisfaction in handling support queries.

[Constraints]: Maintain chatbot's knowledge base, optimize response length, and ensure seamless integration with the support system.

[Style or Tone]: Professional, helpful, and solution-oriented.

[Structure or Format]: Designed conversational interactions for different customer support scenarios.

Prompt: As a Conversational Designer, design conversational interactions for a customer support chatbot in the e-commerce industry. The goal is to improve the chatbot's efficiency and customer satisfaction in handling support queries. Please maintain the chatbot's knowledge base, optimize response length, and ensure seamless integration with the support system, using a professional, helpful, and solution-oriented design style. Provide designed conversational interactions for different customer support scenarios.

17.

[Role]: Conversational Designer
[Task]: Develop a conversational design for a travel booking chatbot assisting users with flight and hotel reservations.
[Context]: The chatbot helps users search for options, compare prices, and make bookings.
[Goal]: Enhance the chatbot's usability and accuracy in providing travel booking services.
[Constraints]: Maintain chatbot's integration with booking platforms, optimize response length, and improve booking success rate.
[Style or Tone]: Informative, efficient, and trustworthy.
[Structure or Format]: Developed conversational design for different travel booking scenarios.

Prompt: As a Conversational Designer, develop a conversational design for a travel booking chatbot assisting users with flight and hotel reservations. The goal is to enhance the chatbot's usability and accuracy in providing travel booking services. Please maintain the chatbot's integration with booking platforms, optimize response length, and improve booking success rate, using an informative, efficient, and trustworthy design style. Provide developed conversational design for different travel booking scenarios.

18.

[Role]: Conversational Designer
[Task]: Design conversational interactions for a virtual assistant chatbot that helps users manage their tasks and schedules.
[Context]: The chatbot offers reminders, scheduling assistance, and task organization features.
[Goal]: Improve the chatbot's effectiveness in aiding users with task management and time optimization.
[Constraints]: Maintain chatbot's task management capabilities, optimize

response length, and enhance user productivity.
[Style or Tone]: Organized, proactive, and reliable.
[Structure or Format]: Designed conversational interactions for different task and schedule management scenarios.

Prompt: As a Conversational Designer, design conversational interactions for a virtual assistant chatbot that helps users manage their tasks and schedules. The goal is to improve the chatbot's effectiveness in aiding users with task management and time optimization. Please maintain the chatbot's task management capabilities, optimize response length, and enhance user productivity, using an organized, proactive, and reliable design style. Provide designed conversational interactions for different task and schedule management scenarios.

19.

[Role]: Conversational Designer
[Task]: Create conversational interactions for a car rental chatbot assisting users with reservations and vehicle information.
[Context]: The chatbot provides rental options, pricing details, and booking confirmations.
[Goal]: Enhance the chatbot's user experience and efficiency in handling car rental inquiries.
[Constraints]: Maintain chatbot's integration with rental services, optimize response length, and improve reservation accuracy.
[Style or Tone]: Informative, friendly, and accommodating.
[Structure or Format]: Created conversational interactions for different car rental scenarios.

Prompt: As a Conversational Designer, create conversational interactions for a car rental chatbot assisting users with reservations and vehicle information. The goal is to enhance the chatbot's user experience and efficiency in handling car rental inquiries. Please maintain the chatbot's integration with rental services, optimize response length, and improve reservation accuracy, using an informative, friendly, and accommodating design style. Provide created conversational interactions for different car rental scenarios.

20.

[Role]: Conversational Designer
[Task]: Design conversational interactions for a health and wellness chatbot offering fitness tips and exercise routines.
[Context]: The chatbot provides personalized workout plans, tracks progress, and offers motivational support.
[Goal]: Improve the chatbot's ability to inspire and guide users towards a healthier lifestyle.
[Constraints]: Maintain chatbot's fitness knowledge, optimize response length, and ensure exercise safety.
[Style or Tone]: Encouraging, supportive, and energetic.
[Structure or Format]: Designed conversational interactions for different fitness activities.

Prompt: As a Conversational Designer, design conversational interactions for a health and wellness chatbot offering fitness tips and exercise routines. The goal is to improve the chatbot's ability to inspire and guide users towards a healthier lifestyle. Please maintain the chatbot's fitness knowledge, optimize response length, and ensure exercise safety, using an encouraging, supportive, and energetic design style. Provide designed conversational interactions for different fitness activities.

21.

[Role]: Conversational Designer
[Task]: Develop conversational interactions for a chatbot that assists users in learning a new programming language.
[Context]: The chatbot provides coding exercises, explanations, and tracks the user's progress.

[Goal]: Enhance the chatbot's effectiveness in facilitating the learning process and improving coding skills.
[Constraints]: Maintain chatbot's programming language knowledge, optimize response length, and promote interactive learning.
[Style or Tone]: Informative, interactive, and supportive.
[Structure or Format]: Developed conversational interactions for different programming concepts and exercises.

Prompt: As a Conversational Designer, develop conversational interactions for a chatbot that assists users in learning a new programming language. The goal is to enhance the chatbot's effectiveness in facilitating the learning process and improving coding skills. Please maintain the chatbot's programming language knowledge, optimize response length, and promote interactive learning, using an informative, interactive, and supportive design style. Provide developed conversational interactions for different programming concepts and exercises.

22.
[Rolc]: Convcrsational Dcsigncr
[Task]: Design conversational interactions for a virtual personal finance advisor chatbot.
[Context]: The chatbot provides budgeting tips, investment advice, and helps users manage their finances.
[Goal]: Improve the chatbot's ability to guide users towards financial stability and informed decision-making.
[Constraints]: Maintain chatbot's financial knowledge, optimize response length, and consider user-specific financial goals.
[Style or Tone]: Informative, practical, and trustworthy.
[Structure or Format]: Designed conversational interactions for different personal finance scenarios.

Prompt: As a Conversational Designer, design conversational interactions for a virtual personal finance advisor chatbot. The goal is to improve the chatbot's ability to guide users towards financial stability and informed decision-making. Please maintain the chatbot's financial knowledge, optimize response length, and consider user-specific financial goals, using an informative, practical, and trustworthy design style. Provide designed conversational interactions for different personal finance scenarios.

23.

[Role]: Conversational Designer
[Task]: Create conversational interactions for a language translation chatbot assisting users in real-time communication.
[Context]: The chatbot translates text and speech between different languages, enabling smooth communication.
[Goal]: Enhance the chatbot's accuracy and efficiency in providing real-time translation services.
[Constraints]: Maintain chatbot's language proficiency, optimize response length, and consider regional language variations.
[Style or Tone]: Clear, concise, and reliable.
[Structure or Format]: Created conversational interactions for different language translation scenarios.

Prompt: As a Conversational Designer, create conversational interactions for a language translation chatbot assisting users in real-time communication. The goal is to enhance the chatbot's accuracy and efficiency in providing real-time translation services. Please maintain the chatbot's language proficiency, optimize response length, and consider regional language variations, using a clear, concise, and reliable design style. Provide created conversational interactions for different language translation scenarios.

24.

[Role]: Conversational Designer
[Task]: Design a natural language flow for a chatbot to handle customer inquiries.
[Context]: Providing an intuitive and helpful conversation experience.
[Goal]: Improve customer satisfaction and reduce support response time.
[Constraints]: Limited response length and adherence to brand tone.
[Style or Tone]: Friendly, helpful, and aligned with the brand persona.
[Structure or Format]: Prepared conversation flow diagrams and sample dialogues.

Prompt: As a Conversational Designer, design a natural language flow for a chatbot to handle customer inquiries. The goal is to improve customer satisfaction and reduce support response time. Please consider the limited response length and adherence to the brand tone, using a friendly, helpful, and brand-aligned style. Provide prepared conversation flow diagrams and sample dialogues.

25.

[Role]: Conversational Designer
[Task]: Develop conversational interactions for a chatbot assisting users in finding and booking restaurant reservations.
[Context]: The chatbot offers restaurant recommendations, availability checks, and reservation confirmations.
[Goal]: Enhance the chatbot's user experience and efficiency in facilitating restaurant bookings.
[Constraints]: Maintain chatbot's integration with reservation platforms, optimize response length, and improve booking success rate.
[Style or Tone]: Informative, friendly, and helpful.
[Structure or Format]: Developed conversational interactions for different restaurant reservation scenarios.

Prompt: As a Conversational Designer, develop conversational interactions for a chatbot assisting users in finding and booking restaurant reservations. The goal is to enhance the chatbot's user experience and efficiency in facilitating restaurant bookings. Please maintain the chatbot's integration with reservation platforms, optimize response length, and improve booking success rate, using an informative, friendly, and helpful design style. Provide developed conversational interactions for different restaurant reservation scenarios.

Prompts for Accessibility Writers

1.

[Role]: Accessibility Writer
[Task]: Create an accessibility guidelines document for a web development team.
[Context]: The team is responsible for designing and developing websites for various clients.
[Goal]: Provide clear instructions and best practices to ensure websites are accessible to users with disabilities.
[Constraints]: Adhere to WCAG 2.1 guidelines, consider different disabilities, and address common accessibility barriers.
[Style or Tone]: Informative, concise, and inclusive.
[Structure or Format]: Prepared an accessibility guidelines document with WCAG 2.1 requirements, accessibility testing methods, and accessible design principles.

Prompt: As an Accessibility Writer, create an accessibility guidelines document for a web development team. The goal is to provide clear instructions and best practices to ensure websites are accessible to users with disabilities. Please adhere to WCAG 2.1 guidelines, consider different disabilities, and address common accessibility barriers, using an informative, concise, and inclusive style. Provide a prepared accessibility guidelines document with WCAG 2.1 requirements, accessibility testing methods, and accessible design principles.

2.

[Role]: Accessibility Writer
[Task]: Write alternative text descriptions for images on a university's e-learning platform.
[Context]: The platform contains a vast library of educational materials, including images, charts, and diagrams.
[Goal]: Ensure visually impaired students can access the content effectively by providing accurate and descriptive alternative text.
[Constraints]: Describe images concisely, provide contextual information, and adhere to accessibility standards.
[Style or Tone]: Clear, concise, and descriptive.
[Structure or Format]: Created alternative text descriptions for images following best practices, including image captions and long descriptions where necessary.

Prompt: As an Accessibility Writer, write alternative text descriptions for images on a university's e-learning platform. The goal is to ensure visually impaired students can access the content effectively by providing accurate and descriptive alternative text. Please describe images concisely, provide contextual information, and adhere to accessibility standards, using a clear, concise, and descriptive style. Provide alternative text descriptions for images following best practices, including image captions and long descriptions where necessary.

3.

[Role]: Accessibility Writer
[Task]: Review and enhance the closed captioning for a series of instructional videos.
[Context]: The videos are educational tutorials for an online learning platform.
[Goal]: Improve the accessibility of the videos by ensuring accurate and synchronized closed captions.
[Constraints]: Review and edit existing captions, ensure proper timing, and address any errors or inaccuracies.

[Style or Tone]: Clear, readable, and synchronized with the audio.
[Structure or Format]: Revised closed captioning for the videos, including accurate transcriptions and synchronized timing.

Prompt: As an Accessibility Writer, review and enhance the closed captioning for a series of instructional videos. The goal is to improve the accessibility of the videos by ensuring accurate and synchronized closed captions. Please review and edit existing captions, ensure proper timing, and address any errors or inaccuracies, using a clear, readable, and synchronized style. Provide revised closed captioning for the videos, including accurate transcriptions and synchronized timing.

4.
[Role]: Accessibility Writer
[Task]: Develop an accessibility statement for a government agency's website.
[Context]: The website provides information and services to the public.
[Goal]: Communicate the agency's commitment to accessibility and inform users about available accommodations.
[Constraints]: Include relevant legal requirements, address common accessibility barriers, and provide contact information for accessibility inquiries.
[Style or Tone]: Informative, transparent, and user-focused.
[Structure or Format]: Prepared an accessibility statement with the agency's accessibility policy, available accommodations, and contact details.

Prompt: As an Accessibility Writer, develop an accessibility statement for a government agency's website. The goal is to communicate the agency's commitment to accessibility and inform users about available accommodations. Please include relevant legal requirements, address common accessibility barriers, and provide contact information for accessibility inquiries, using an informative, transparent, and user-focused style. Provide a prepared accessibility statement with the agency's accessibility policy, available accommodations, and contact details.

5.

[Role]: Accessibility Writer
[Task]: Create an accessible user manual for a mobile application.
[Context]: The application helps users track their fitness goals and offers various features and functionalities.
[Goal]: Provide step-by-step instructions that are accessible to users with different disabilities.
[Constraints]: Use plain language, provide alternative formats, and address specific accessibility considerations.
[Style or Tone]: User-friendly, concise, and inclusive.
[Structure or Format]: Developed an accessible user manual with clear instructions, alternative text for visuals, and assistive technology recommendations.

Prompt: As an Accessibility Writer, create an accessible user manual for a mobile application. The goal is to provide step-by-step instructions that are accessible to users with different disabilities. Please use plain language, provide alternative formats, and address specific accessibility considerations, using a user-friendly, concise, and inclusive style. Provide a developed accessible user manual with clear instructions, alternative text for visuals, and assistive technology recommendations.

6.

[Role]: Accessibility Writer
[Task]: Conduct an accessibility audit of a company's website.
[Context]: The website is a critical touchpoint for the company's online presence and user interactions.
[Goal]: Identify accessibility issues and provide recommendations for improvement.
[Constraints]: Follow WCAG 2.1 guidelines, test on different devices and assistive technologies, and prioritize the most impactful issues.
[Style or Tone]: Detailed, comprehensive, and actionable.
[Structure or Format]: Produced an accessibility audit report with identified issues, severity levels, and suggested remediation steps.

Prompt: As an Accessibility Writer, conduct an accessibility audit of a company's website. The goal is to identify accessibility issues and provide recommendations for improvement. Please follow WCAG 2.1 guidelines, test on different devices and assistive technologies, and prioritize the most impactful issues, using a detailed, comprehensive, and actionable style. Provide an accessibility audit report with identified issues, severity levels, and suggested remediation steps.

7.

[Role]: Accessibility Writer
[Task]: Create a set of accessibility guidelines for social media content.
[Context]: The organization uses social media platforms to engage with its audience and share information.
[Goal]: Ensure that social media content is accessible to users with disabilities.
[Constraints]: Consider platform-specific accessibility features, provide alternative text for visuals, and address captioning for videos.
[Style or Tone]: Informative, concise, and platform-specific.
[Structure or Format]: Developed accessibility guidelines with platform-specific recommendations, alternative text guidelines, and captioning requirements.

Prompt: As an Accessibility Writer, create a set of accessibility guidelines for social media content. The goal is to ensure that social media content is accessible to users with disabilities. Please consider platform-specific accessibility features, provide alternative text for visuals, and address captioning for videos, using an informative, concise, and platform-specific style. Provide developed accessibility guidelines with platform-specific recommendations, alternative text guidelines, and captioning requirements.

8.

[Role]: Accessibility Writer

[Task]: Review and update the alt text descriptions for a library's digital image collection.

[Context]: The library's digital collection contains diverse images representing various subjects and historical artifacts.

[Goal]: Enhance the accessibility and inclusivity of the digital collection by providing accurate and descriptive alt text.

[Constraints]: Follow best practices for alt text, collaborate with subject matter experts, and ensure consistency across images.

[Style or Tone]: Descriptive, informative, and culturally sensitive.

[Structure or Format]: Revised alt text descriptions for the images, including accurate and descriptive information.

Prompt: As an Accessibility Writer, review and update the alt text descriptions for a library's digital image collection. The goal is to enhance the accessibility and inclusivity of the digital collection by providing accurate and descriptive alt text. Please follow best practices for alt text, collaborate with subject matter experts, and ensure consistency across images, using a descriptive, informative, and culturally sensitive style. Provide revised alt text descriptions for the images, including accurate and descriptive information.

9.

[Role]: Accessibility Writer

[Task]: Develop a style guide for creating accessible PDF documents.

[Context]: The organization frequently creates PDF documents for sharing information and resources.

[Goal]: Ensure that PDF documents are accessible to users with disabilities, including proper document structure and text formatting.

[Constraints]: Consider assistive technology compatibility, provide guidance on headings and alternative text, and address color contrast requirements.

[Style or Tone]: Clear, instructional, and comprehensive.
[Structure or Format]: Created a style guide with step-by-step instructions, accessibility checklists, and examples for creating accessible PDF documents.

Prompt: As an Accessibility Writer, develop a style guide for creating accessible PDF documents. The goal is to ensure that PDF documents are accessible to users with disabilities, including proper document structure and text formatting. Please consider assistive technology compatibility, provide guidance on headings and alternative text, and address color contrast requirements, using a clear, instructional, and comprehensive style. Provide a created style guide with step-by-step instructions, accessibility checklists, and examples for creating accessible PDF documents.

10.
[Role]: Accessibility Writer
[Task]: Conduct a training session on inclusive writing for a content team.
[Context]: The content team is responsible for creating various types of written content for a website.
[Goal]: Promote inclusive language and ensure content is accessible to diverse audiences.
[Constraints]: Address bias, consider readability and plain language, and provide practical examples and exercises.
[Style or Tone]: Engaging, interactive, and inclusive.
[Structure or Format]: Conducted a training session with presentation slides, interactive activities, and handouts for inclusive writing.

Prompt: As an Accessibility Writer, conduct a training session on inclusive writing for a content team. The goal is to promote inclusive language and ensure content is accessible to diverse audiences. Please address bias, consider readability and plain language, and provide practical examples and exercises, using an engaging, interactive, and inclusive style.

Conduct a training session with presentation slides, interactive activities, and handouts for inclusive writing.

11.

[Role]: Accessibility Writer
[Task]: Develop an accessibility checklist for website content creators.
[Context]: The organization has multiple content creators responsible for publishing content on the website.
[Goal]: Provide a comprehensive checklist to ensure all content meets accessibility standards.
[Constraints]: Cover key accessibility elements such as headings, alternative text, color contrast, and keyboard navigation.
[Style or Tone]: Clear, concise, and user-friendly.
[Structure or Format]: Created an accessibility checklist with actionable items, explanations, and references for website content creators.

Prompt: As an Accessibility Writer, develop an accessibility checklist for website content creators. The goal is to provide a comprehensive checklist to ensure all content meets accessibility standards. Please cover key accessibility elements such as headings, alternative text, color contrast, and keyboard navigation, using a clear, concise, and user-friendly style. Provide a created accessibility checklist with actionable items, explanations, and references for website content creators.

12.

[Role]: Accessibility Writer
[Task]: Conduct a usability test for a mobile app from an accessibility perspective.
[Context]: The mobile app provides a range of features and functionalities to users.
[Goal]: Identify usability issues for users with disabilities and provide actionable recommendations.

[Constraints]: Test on various assistive technologies, follow WCAG guidelines, and consider user feedback.
[Style or Tone]: Detailed, objective, and solution-oriented.
[Structure or Format]: Conducted a usability test report with findings, recommendations, and prioritized action items.

Prompt: As an Accessibility Writer, conduct a usability test for a mobile app from an accessibility perspective. The goal is to identify usability issues for users with disabilities and provide actionable recommendations. Please test on various assistive technologies, follow WCAG guidelines, and consider user feedback, using a detailed, objective, and solution-oriented style. Provide a conducted usability test report with findings, recommendations, and prioritized action items.

13.
[Role]: Accessibility Writer
[Task]: Create a set of guidelines for designing accessible forms.
[Context]: The organization's website contains forms for various purposes, such as contact forms and registration forms.
[Goal]: Ensure forms are accessible and usable for all users, including those with disabilities.
[Constraints]: Cover form labels, input validation, error messaging, and assistive technology compatibility.
[Style or Tone]: Informative, practical, and user-centered.
[Structure or Format]: Developed a set of guidelines with examples, best practices, and considerations for designing accessible forms.

Prompt: As an Accessibility Writer, create a set of guidelines for designing accessible forms. The goal is to ensure forms are accessible and usable for all users, including those with disabilities. Please cover form labels, input validation, error messaging, and assistive technology compatibility, using an informative, practical, and user-centered style. Provide a developed set of guidelines with examples, best practices, and considerations for designing accessible forms.

14.

[Role]: Accessibility Writer
[Task]: Review and revise the transcript for a podcast episode to enhance accessibility.
[Context]: The podcast covers various topics and has a diverse listener base.
[Goal]: Improve the accessibility of the podcast by providing an accurate and detailed transcript.
[Constraints]: Ensure proper punctuation, identify speakers, and address any unclear or inaudible parts.
[Style or Tone]: Clear, readable, and inclusive.
[Structure or Format]: Revised the podcast transcript with accurate timestamps, speaker identifications, and descriptive text.

Prompt: As an Accessibility Writer, review and revise the transcript for a podcast episode to enhance accessibility. The goal is to improve the accessibility of the podcast by providing an accurate and detailed transcript. Please ensure proper punctuation, identify speakers, and address any unclear or inaudible parts, using a clear, readable, and inclusive style. Provide a revised podcast transcript with accurate timestamps, speaker identifications,

15.

[Role]: Accessibility Writer
[Task]: Develop a set of guidelines for creating accessible video content.
[Context]: The organization produces video content for various platforms, including social media and websites.
[Goal]: Ensure that video content is accessible to users with disabilities, including proper captions and audio descriptions.

[Constraints]: Follow accessibility standards (such as WCAG 2.1), provide guidance on captioning and audio description techniques, and consider different video formats and players.
[Style or Tone]: Informative, instructional, and comprehensive.
[Structure or Format]: Created a set of guidelines with step-by-step instructions, best practices, and examples for creating accessible video content.

Prompt: As an Accessibility Writer, develop a set of guidelines for creating accessible video content. The goal is to ensure that video content is accessible to users with disabilities, including proper captions and audio descriptions. Please follow accessibility standards (such as WCAG 2.1), provide guidance on captioning and audio description techniques, and consider different video formats and players, using an informative, instructional, and comprehensive style. Provide a created set of guidelines with step-by-step instructions, best practices, and examples for creating accessible video content.

16.

[Role]: Accessibility Writer
[Task]: Review and revise the alt text for a collection of images on a website.
[Context]: The website contains images related to products, services, and company events.
[Goal]: Enhance the accessibility of the website by providing accurate and descriptive alt text for images.
[Constraints]: Follow best practices for alt text, ensure consistency in tone and style, and consider the context of each image.
[Style or Tone]: Descriptive, concise, and user-focused.
[Structure or Format]: Revised the alt text for the images, including accurate descriptions and keywords.

Prompt: As an Accessibility Writer, review and revise the alt text for a collection of images on a website. The goal is to enhance the accessibility of the website by providing accurate and descriptive alt text for images. Please follow best practices for alt text, ensure consistency in tone and style, and consider the context of each image, using a descriptive, concise, and user-focused style. Provide revised alt text for the images, including accurate descriptions and keywords.

17.

[Role]: Accessibility Writer
[Task]: Conduct an accessibility review of a mobile app's navigation menu.
[Context]: The mobile app has a complex navigation structure with multiple menu options.
[Goal]: Identify accessibility barriers and provide recommendations for improving the navigation menu's usability.
[Constraints]: Test the navigation menu using different assistive technologies, consider touch gestures and keyboard navigation, and follow accessibility guidelines.
[Style or Tone]: Detailed, actionable, and user-centered.
[Structure or Format]: Conducted an accessibility review report with findings, recommendations, and prioritized action items for the navigation menu.

Prompt: As an Accessibility Writer, conduct an accessibility review of a mobile app's navigation menu. The goal is to identify accessibility barriers and provide recommendations for improving the navigation menu's usability. Please test the navigation menu using different assistive technologies, consider touch gestures and keyboard navigation, and follow accessibility guidelines, using a detailed, actionable, and user-centered style. Provide a conducted accessibility review report with findings, recommendations, and prioritized action items for the navigation menu.

18.

[Role]: Accessibility Writer
[Task]: Develop a set of guidelines for creating accessible infographics.
[Context]: The organization frequently creates infographics to visually communicate information.
[Goal]: Ensure that infographics are accessible and convey information effectively to users with disabilities.
[Constraints]: Provide guidance on color contrast, use of text alternatives, and proper information hierarchy.
[Style or Tone]: Informative, visual, and easy to follow.
[Structure or Format]: Created a set of guidelines with best practices, tips, and examples for creating accessible infographics.

Prompt: As an Accessibility Writer, develop a set of guidelines for creating accessible infographics. The goal is to ensure that infographics are accessible and convey information effectively to users with disabilities. Please provide guidance on color contrast, use of text alternatives, and proper information hierarchy, using an informative, visual, and easy-to-follow style. Provide a created set of guidelines with best practices, tips, and examples for creating accessible infographics.

19.

[Role]: Accessibility Writer
[Task]: Conduct an accessibility audit of a website's navigation structure.
[Context]: The website has multiple sections and a hierarchical navigation menu.
[Goal]: Identify navigation-related accessibility issues and provide recommendations for improvement.
[Constraints]: Follow accessibility standards (such as WCAG 2.1), consider keyboard navigation, and address issues like focus management and logical information architecture.
[Style or Tone]: Detailed, comprehensive, and solution-oriented.

[Structure or Format]: Conducted an accessibility audit report with findings, recommendations, and actionable steps for the website's navigation structure.

Prompt: As an Accessibility Writer, conduct an accessibility audit of a website's navigation structure. The goal is to identify navigation-related accessibility issues and provide recommendations for improvement. Please follow accessibility standards (such as WCAG 2.1), consider keyboard navigation, and address issues like focus management and logical information architecture, using a detailed, comprehensive, and solution-oriented style. Provide a conducted accessibility audit report with findings, recommendations, and actionable steps for the website's navigation structure.

20.

[Role]: Accessibility Writer
[Task]: Develop a style guide for creating accessible social media posts.
[Context]: The organization regularly publishes social media content across various platforms.
[Goal]: Ensure that social media posts are accessible and inclusive to a wide range of users.
[Constraints]: Cover elements like image descriptions, alt text, captioning, and readability.
[Style or Tone]: Clear, concise, and engaging.
[Structure or Format]: Created a style guide with examples, guidelines, and tips for creating accessible social media posts.

Prompt: As an Accessibility Writer, develop a style guide for creating accessible social media posts. The goal is to ensure that social media posts are accessible and inclusive to a wide range of users. Please cover elements like image descriptions, alt text, captioning, and readability, using a clear, concise, and engaging style. Provide a created style guide with examples, guidelines, and tips for creating accessible social media posts.

21.

[Role]: Accessibility Writer
[Task]: Conduct an accessibility review of a website's color palette.
[Context]: The website uses various colors for branding and visual elements.
[Goal]: Identify any color-related accessibility issues and provide recommendations for improvement.
[Constraints]: Follow color contrast guidelines, consider color blindness and visual impairments, and suggest alternative color options.
[Style or Tone]: Detailed, informative, and user-centered.
[Structure or Format]: Conducted an accessibility review report with findings, recommendations, and color contrast analysis for the website's color palette.

Prompt: As an Accessibility Writer, conduct an accessibility review of a website's color palette. The goal is to identify any color-related accessibility issues and provide recommendations for improvement. Please follow color contrast guidelines, consider color blindness and visual impairments, and suggest alternative color options, using a detailed, informative, and user-centered style. Provide a conducted accessibility review report with findings, recommendations, and color contrast analysis for the website's color palette.

22.

[Role]: Accessibility Writer
[Task]: Create an accessibility training program for content creators.
[Context]: The organization has a team of content creators responsible for producing digital content.
[Goal]: Educate content creators about accessibility best practices and guidelines.
[Constraints]: Cover topics like inclusive writing, alternative text, headings, and document structure.
[Style or Tone]: Engaging, interactive, and informative.

[Structure or Format]: Developed an accessibility training program with modules, presentations, exercises, and quizzes for content creators.

Prompt: As an Accessibility Writer, create an accessibility training program for content creators. The goal is to educate content creators about accessibility best practices and guidelines. Please cover topics like inclusive writing, alternative text, headings, and document structure, using an engaging, interactive, and informative style. Provide a developed accessibility training program with modules, presentations, exercises, and quizzes for content creators.

23.

[Role]: Accessibility Writer

[Task]: Conduct an accessibility evaluation of a digital document.

[Context]: The digital document contains text, images, tables, and other visual elements.

[Goal]: Identify accessibility barriers and provide recommendations for improving the document's accessibility.

[Constraints]: Follow accessibility standards, consider screen reader compatibility, provide proper alternative text, and ensure proper heading structure.

[Style or Tone]: Detailed, objective, and actionable.

[Structure or Format]: Conducted an accessibility evaluation report with findings, recommendations, and guidelines for improving the document's accessibility.

Prompt: As an Accessibility Writer, conduct an accessibility evaluation of a digital document. The goal is to identify accessibility barriers and provide recommendations for improving the document's accessibility. Please follow accessibility standards, consider screen reader compatibility, provide proper alternative text, and ensure proper heading structure, using a detailed, objective, and actionable style. Provide a conducted accessibility evaluation report with findings, recommendations, and guidelines for improving the document's accessibility.

24.

[Role]: Accessibility Writer
[Task]: Develop a checklist for evaluating the accessibility of web forms.
[Context]: The organization's website contains various forms for user interaction.
[Goal]: Ensure that web forms are accessible and easy to use for all users.
[Constraints]: Consider keyboard navigation, form labels, error messaging, and ARIA attributes.
[Style or Tone]: Concise, organized, and user-friendly.
[Structure or Format]: Created a checklist with step-by-step evaluation criteria, tips, and best practices for assessing the accessibility of web forms.

Prompt: As an Accessibility Writer, develop a checklist for evaluating the accessibility of web forms. The goal is to ensure that web forms are accessible and easy to use for all users. Please consider keyboard navigation, form labels, error messaging, and ARIA attributes, using a concise, organized, and user-friendly style. Provide a created checklist with step-by-step evaluation criteria, tips, and best practices for assessing the accessibility of web forms.

25.

[Role]: Accessibility Writer
[Task]: Review and revise content to ensure compliance with accessibility guidelines.
[Context]: Ensuring content is accessible to users with disabilities.
[Goal]: Improve inclusivity and usability for all users.
[Constraints]: Follow accessibility standards and guidelines.
[Style or Tone]: Clear, concise, and inclusive.
[Structure or Format]: Prepared accessibility content review reports.

Prompt: As an Accessibility Writer, review and revise content to ensure compliance with accessibility guidelines. The goal is to improve inclusivity and usability for all users. Please follow accessibility standards and guidelines, using a clear, concise, and inclusive style. Provide prepared accessibility content review reports.

Prompts for Content Strategists

1.

[Role]: Content Strategist
[Task]: Develop a content strategy for a fashion e-commerce website targeting millennials.
[Context]: The website offers trendy clothing, accessories, and fashion tips.
[Goal]: Increase website traffic, engage the target audience, and drive conversions.
[Constraints]: Align with brand voice, consider SEO best practices, and cater to millennial preferences.
[Style or Tone]: Trendy, relatable, and aspirational.
[Structure or Format]: Created content strategy outlining topic clusters, target keywords, and content types.

Prompt: As a Content Strategist, develop a content strategy for a fashion e-commerce website targeting millennials. The goal is to increase website traffic, engage the target audience, and drive conversions. Please align with the brand voice, consider SEO best practices, and cater to millennial preferences, using a trendy, relatable, and aspirational style. Provide a created content strategy outlining topic clusters, target keywords, and content types.

2.

[Role]: Content Strategist
[Task]: Create a content calendar for a technology blog targeting professionals in the IT industry.
[Context]: The blog covers emerging technologies, industry trends, and best practices.

[Goal]: Establish thought leadership, provide valuable insights, and increase reader engagement.
[Constraints]: Maintain editorial consistency, adhere to publishing schedule, and incorporate SEO strategies.
[Style or Tone]: Informative, authoritative, and approachable.
[Structure or Format]: Designed a content calendar with topics, publication dates, and content formats.

Prompt: As a Content Strategist, create a content calendar for a technology blog targeting professionals in the IT industry. The goal is to establish thought leadership, provide valuable insights, and increase reader engagement. Please maintain editorial consistency, adhere to the publishing schedule, and incorporate SEO strategies, using an informative, authoritative, and approachable style. Provide a designed content calendar with topics, publication dates, and content formats.

3.
[Role]: Content Strategist
[Task]: Develop a content distribution plan for a B2B software company targeting enterprise-level customers.
[Context]: The company offers specialized software solutions for business automation.
[Goal]: Increase brand visibility, generate leads, and nurture customer relationships.
[Constraints]: Align with company's value proposition, leverage relevant channels, and focus on industry-specific content.
[Style or Tone]: Professional, informative, and persuasive.
[Structure or Format]: Created a content distribution plan outlining channels, messaging, and engagement strategies.

Prompt: As a Content Strategist, develop a content distribution plan for a B2B software company targeting enterprise-level customers. The goal is to increase brand visibility, generate leads, and nurture customer relationships.

Please align with the company's value proposition, leverage relevant channels, and focus on industry-specific content, using a professional, informative, and persuasive style. Provide a created content distribution plan outlining channels, messaging, and engagement strategies.

4.

[Role]: Content Strategist
[Task]: Design a content framework for a lifestyle blog catering to health-conscious individuals.
[Context]: The blog covers topics like fitness, nutrition, mental wellness, and holistic living.
[Goal]: Inspire and educate readers, encourage healthy lifestyle choices, and build a loyal community.
[Constraints]: Maintain a balanced content mix, incorporate personal anecdotes, and adhere to the blog's tone.
[Style or Tone]: Inspirational, informative, and relatable.
[Structure or Format]: Designed a content framework with categories, subtopics, and content angles.

Prompt: As a Content Strategist, design a content framework for a lifestyle blog catering to health-conscious individuals. The goal is to inspire and educate readers, encourage healthy lifestyle choices, and build a loyal community. Please maintain a balanced content mix, incorporate personal anecdotes, and adhere to the blog's tone, using an inspirational, informative, and relatable style. Provide a designed content framework with categories, subtopics, and content angles.

5.

[Role]: Content Strategist
[Task]: Develop a social media content strategy for a travel agency targeting adventure enthusiasts.
[Context]: The agency offers adventure travel packages and experiences.
[Goal]: Increase brand awareness, drive engagement, and attract adventure-seeking customers.

[Constraints]: Align with brand identity, optimize content for different platforms, and incorporate user-generated content.
[Style or Tone]: Adventurous, inspiring, and shareable.
[Structure or Format]: Created a social media content strategy with post themes, hashtags, and visual guidelines.

Prompt: As a Content Strategist, develop a social media content strategy for a travel agency targeting adventure enthusiasts. The goal is to increase brand awareness, drive engagement, and attract adventure-seeking customers. Please align with the brand identity, optimize content for different platforms, and incorporate user-generated content, using an adventurous, inspiring, and shareable style. Provide a created social media content strategy with post themes, hashtags, and visual guidelines.

6.
[Role]: Content Strategist
[Task]: Create an email marketing strategy for a subscription-based beauty box service.
[Context]: The service delivers curated beauty products to subscribers on a monthly basis.
[Goal]: Increase email open rates, drive subscription renewals, and foster customer loyalty.
[Constraints]: Adhere to brand guidelines, optimize subject lines for engagement, and segment the email list.
[Style or Tone]: Personalized, informative, and enticing.
[Structure or Format]: Developed an email marketing strategy with content themes, call-to-action strategies, and A/B testing plans.

Prompt: As a Content Strategist, create an email marketing strategy for a subscription-based beauty box service. The goal is to increase email open rates, drive subscription renewals, and foster customer loyalty. Please adhere to brand guidelines, optimize subject lines for engagement, and segment the email list, using a personalized, informative, and enticing style. Provide a developed email marketing strategy with content themes, call-to-action strategies, and A/B testing plans.

7.

[Role]: Content Strategist
[Task]: Develop a content curation plan for a news website targeting tech-savvy readers.
[Context]: The website covers the latest news in the tech industry.
[Goal]: Provide readers with relevant, high-quality news articles and keep them informed about tech trends.
[Constraints]: Consider copyright and fair use guidelines, curate from reputable sources, and offer diverse perspectives.
[Style or Tone]: Objective, timely, and engaging.
[Structure or Format]: Created a content curation plan with topic categories, trusted sources, and editorial guidelines.

Prompt: As a Content Strategist, develop a content curation plan for a news website targeting tech-savvy readers. The goal is to provide readers with relevant, high-quality news articles and keep them informed about tech trends. Please consider copyright and fair use guidelines, curate from reputable sources, and offer diverse perspectives, using an objective, timely, and engaging style. Provide a created content curation plan with topic categories, trusted sources, and editorial guidelines.

8.

[Role]: Content Strategist
[Task]: Design a content localization strategy for a global e-commerce platform.
[Context]: The platform sells products internationally in multiple languages.
[Goal]: Provide a seamless user experience and engage customers across different regions.

[Constraints]: Maintain brand consistency, consider cultural sensitivities, and optimize content for local search engines.
[Style or Tone]: Culturally sensitive, persuasive, and conversion-focused.
[Structure or Format]: Designed a content localization strategy with translation workflows, localization guidelines, and SEO tactics.

Prompt: As a Content Strategist, design a content localization strategy for a global e-commerce platform. The goal is to provide a seamless user experience and engage customers across different regions. Please maintain brand consistency, consider cultural sensitivities, and optimize content for local search engines, using a culturally sensitive, persuasive, and conversion-focused style. Provide a designed content localization strategy with translation workflows, localization guidelines, and SEO tactics.

9.
[Role]: Content Strategist
[Task]: Develop a content engagement plan for a nonprofit organization's website.
[Context]: The organization focuses on environmental conservation and sustainable practices.
[Goal]: Increase visitor engagement, encourage donations, and raise awareness about environmental issues.
[Constraints]: Align with the organization's mission, leverage storytelling techniques, and incorporate multimedia content.
[Style or Tone]: Inspiring, educational, and impactful.
[Structure or Format]: Developed a content engagement plan with interactive elements, storytelling frameworks, and donation call-to-action strategies.

Prompt: As a Content Strategist, develop a content engagement plan for a nonprofit organization's website. The goal is to increase visitor engagement, encourage donations, and raise awareness about environmental issues. Please align with the organization's mission, leverage storytelling techniques

10.

[Role]: Content Strategist
[Task]: Create a content governance framework for a large-scale e-learning platform.
[Context]: The platform offers online courses across various disciplines.
[Goal]: Ensure content consistency, quality, and relevance across the platform.
[Constraints]: Establish content review processes, adhere to accessibility guidelines, and accommodate user feedback.
[Style or Tone]: Clear, organized, and authoritative.
[Structure or Format]: Designed a content governance framework with content guidelines, approval workflows, and quality assurance procedures.

Prompt: As a Content Strategist, create a content governance framework for a large-scale e-learning platform. The goal is to ensure content consistency, quality, and relevance across the platform. Please establish content review processes, adhere to accessibility guidelines, and accommodate user feedback, using a clear, organized, and authoritative style. Provide a designed content governance framework with content guidelines, approval workflows, and quality assurance procedures.

11.

[Role]: Content Strategist
[Task]: Develop a content amplification strategy for a startup's blog targeting industry professionals.
[Context]: The blog covers insights and thought leadership in a specific niche.
[Goal]: Increase blog reach, attract industry influencers, and drive traffic to the website.
[Constraints]: Consider budget limitations, leverage social media channels, and explore guest posting opportunities.
[Style or Tone]: Professional, informative, and shareable.

[Structure or Format]: Created a content amplification strategy with targeted distribution channels, influencer outreach plans, and promotional tactics.

Prompt: As a Content Strategist, develop a content amplification strategy for a startup's blog targeting industry professionals. The goal is to increase blog reach, attract industry influencers, and drive traffic to the website. Please consider budget limitations, leverage social media channels, and explore guest posting opportunities, using a professional, informative, and shareable style. Provide a created content amplification strategy with targeted distribution channels, influencer outreach plans, and promotional tactics.

12.
[Role]: Content Strategist
[Task]: Design a content collaboration framework for a cross-functional marketing team.
[Context]: The team consists of members from different marketing disciplines.
[Goal]: Foster collaboration, streamline content creation processes, and maximize team efficiency.
[Constraints]: Establish clear roles and responsibilities, leverage collaboration tools, and optimize workflow integration.
[Style or Tone]: Collaborative, efficient, and transparent.
[Structure or Format]: Designed a content collaboration framework with defined roles, communication channels, and project management tools.

Prompt: As a Content Strategist, design a content collaboration framework for a cross-functional marketing team. The goal is to foster collaboration, streamline content creation processes, and maximize team efficiency. Please establish clear roles and responsibilities, leverage collaboration tools, and optimize workflow integration, using a collaborative, efficient, and transparent style. Provide a designed content collaboration framework with defined roles, communication channels, and project management tools.

13.
[Role]: Content Strategist
[Task]: Develop a content personalization strategy for an e-commerce website selling personalized gifts.
[Context]: The website offers customizable products for various occasions.
[Goal]: Enhance user experience, improve conversion rates, and increase customer satisfaction.
[Constraints]: Utilize customer data, implement personalization algorithms, and ensure data privacy compliance.
[Style or Tone]: Personalized, engaging, and persuasive.
[Structure or Format]: Developed a content personalization strategy with user segmentation, personalized product recommendations, and dynamic content implementation.

Prompt: As a Content Strategist, develop a content personalization strategy for an e-commerce website selling personalized gifts. The goal is to enhance user experience, improve conversion rates, and increase customer satisfaction. Please utilize customer data, implement personalization algorithms, and ensure data privacy compliance, using a personalized, engaging, and persuasive style. Provide a developed content personalization strategy with user segmentation, personalized product recommendations, and dynamic content implementation.

14.
[Role]: Content Strategist
[Task]: Create a brand voice and tone guide for a software company targeting enterprise clients.
[Context]: The company provides enterprise-level software solutions.

[Goal]: Establish a consistent brand voice, enhance brand perception, and resonate with the target audience.
[Constraints]: Consider industry standards, align with company values, and accommodate different communication channels.
[Style or Tone]: Professional, authoritative, and trustworthy.
[Structure or Format]: Designed a brand voice and tone guide with brand personality attributes, writing guidelines, and tone examples.

Prompt: As a Content Strategist, create a brand voice and tone guide for a software company targeting enterprise clients. The goal is to establish a consistent brand voice, enhance brand perception, and resonate with the target audience. Please consider industry standards, align with company values, and accommodate different communication channels, using a professional, authoritative, and trustworthy style. Provide a designed brand voice and tone guide with brand personality attributes, writing guidelines, and tone examples.

15.
[Role]: Content Strategist
[Task]: Develop a thought leadership content strategy for a B2B technology company.
[Context]: The company specializes in providing cutting-edge technology solutions to businesses.
[Goal]: Position the company as an industry leader, attract high-value leads, and drive conversions.
[Constraints]: Align with target audience interests, research industry trends, and incorporate data-driven insights.
[Style or Tone]: Insightful, authoritative, and forward-thinking.
[Structure or Format]: Created a thought leadership content strategy with topic clusters, expert interviews, and distribution plans.

Prompt: As a Content Strategist, develop a thought leadership content strategy for a B2B technology company. The goal is to position the company as an industry leader, attract high-value leads, and drive conversions. Please align with target audience interests, research industry trends, and incorporate data-driven insights, using an insightful, authoritative, and forward-thinking style. Provide a created thought leadership content strategy with topic clusters, expert interviews, and distribution plans.

16.

[Role]: Content Strategist
[Task]: Create a content optimization plan for a SaaS company's website to improve organic search rankings.
[Context]: The company offers software-as-a-service solutions in a competitive market.
[Goal]: Increase website visibility, drive organic traffic, and generate leads.
[Constraints]: Conduct keyword research, optimize on-page elements, and improve website loading speed.
[Style or Tone]: Informative, concise, and keyword-focused.
[Structure or Format]: Designed a content optimization plan with SEO recommendations, meta tag optimizations, and content restructuring guidelines.

Prompt: As a Content Strategist, create a content optimization plan for a SaaS company's website to improve organic search rankings. The goal is to increase website visibility, drive organic traffic, and generate leads. Please conduct keyword research, optimize on-page elements, and improve website loading speed, using an informative, concise, and keyword-focused style. Provide a designed content optimization plan with SEO recommendations, meta tag optimizations, and content restructuring guidelines.

17.

[Role]: Content Strategist
[Task]: Develop a content syndication strategy for a media company's online publication.
[Context]: The publication covers various topics and attracts a large readership.
[Goal]: Expand content reach, increase brand exposure, and drive traffic to the website.
[Constraints]: Identify suitable content syndication platforms, optimize content for syndication, and track performance metrics.
[Style or Tone]: Engaging, shareable, and consistent with the publication's brand.
[Structure or Format]: Developed a content syndication strategy with target platforms, content repurposing tactics, and performance measurement methods.

Prompt: As a Content Strategist, develop a content syndication strategy for a media company's online publication. The goal is to expand content reach, increase brand exposure, and drive traffic to the website. Please identify suitable content syndication platforms, optimize content for syndication, and track performance metrics, using an engaging, shareable, and consistent style with the publication's brand. Provide a developed content syndication strategy with target platforms, content repurposing tactics, and performance measurement methods.

18.

[Role]: Content Strategist
[Task]: Design an onboarding content plan for a mobile app targeting new users.
[Context]: The app provides a unique service to help users achieve a specific goal.
[Goal]: Provide a seamless onboarding experience, educate users about the

app's features, and encourage app engagement.
[Constraints]: Use interactive elements, consider user feedback, and personalize the onboarding experience.
[Style or Tone]: User-friendly, informative, and motivating.
[Structure or Format]: Designed an onboarding content plan with step-by-step tutorials, interactive walkthroughs, and in-app notifications.

Prompt: As a Content Strategist, design an onboarding content plan for a mobile app targeting new users. The goal is to provide a seamless onboarding experience, educate users about the app's features, and encourage app engagement. Please use interactive elements, consider user feedback, and personalize the onboarding experience, using a user-friendly, informative, and motivating style. Provide a designed onboarding content plan with step-by-step tutorials, interactive walkthroughs, and in-app notifications.

19.

[Role]: Content Strategist
[Task]: Create a content distribution strategy for a travel company's blog.
[Context]: The blog features travel guides, tips, and destination recommendations.
[Goal]: Increase blog readership, attract travel enthusiasts, and drive bookings.
[Constraints]: Identify relevant online communities, leverage social media platforms, and collaborate with travel influencers.
[Style or Tone]: Inspirational, informative, and visually appealing.
[Structure or Format]: Created a content distribution strategy with social media content calendars, influencer partnership plans, and community engagement tactics.

Prompt: As a Content Strategist, create a content distribution strategy for a travel company's blog. The goal is to increase blog readership, attract travel enthusiasts, and drive bookings. Please identify relevant online communities, leverage social media platforms, and collaborate with travel influencers, using an inspirational, informative, and visually appealing style. Provide a created content distribution strategy with social media content calendars, influencer partnership plans, and community engagement tactics.

20.

[Role]: Content Strategist
[Task]: Develop a content curation strategy for a fashion e-commerce platform's blog.
[Context]: The blog covers fashion trends, style tips, and brand spotlights.
[Goal]: Provide valuable and curated content to engage fashion enthusiasts, drive website traffic, and increase conversions.
[Constraints]: Curate from reputable sources, maintain a consistent brand voice, and include visual elements.
[Style or Tone]: Trendy, informative, and visually appealing.
[Structure or Format]: Developed a content curation strategy with curated content sources, editorial guidelines, and visual storytelling elements.

Prompt: As a Content Strategist, develop a content curation strategy for a fashion e-commerce platform's blog. The goal is to provide valuable and curated content to engage fashion enthusiasts, drive website traffic, and increase conversions. Please curate from reputable sources, maintain a consistent brand voice, and include visual elements, using a trendy, informative, and visually appealing style. Provide a developed content curation strategy with curated content sources, editorial guidelines, and visual storytelling elements.

21.

[Role]: Content Strategist
[Task]: Design a content calendar for a social media marketing agency's clients.

[Context]: The agency manages social media accounts for various businesses across different industries.
[Goal]: Plan and schedule engaging and relevant social media content to increase brand visibility and audience engagement.
[Constraints]: Consider client preferences, align with marketing campaigns, and optimize posting frequency.
[Style or Tone]: Captivating, shareable, and tailored to the target audience.
[Structure or Format]: Designed a content calendar with monthly themes, content categories, and post scheduling.

Prompt: As a Content Strategist, design a content calendar for a social media marketing agency's clients. The goal is to plan and schedule engaging and relevant social media content to increase brand visibility and audience engagement. Please consider client preferences, align with marketing campaigns, and optimize posting frequency, using a captivating, shareable, and tailored style to the target audience. Provide a designed content calendar with monthly themes, content categories, and post scheduling.

22.
[Role]: Content Strategist
[Task]: Create a brand storytelling strategy for a nonprofit organization.
[Context]: The organization focuses on a specific cause and aims to raise awareness and donations.
[Goal]: Communicate the organization's mission, impact, and stories to connect with the audience and inspire action.
[Constraints]: Highlight real-life stories, maintain authenticity, and adhere to the organization's values.
[Style or Tone]: Emotional, compelling, and authentic.
[Structure or Format]: Created a brand storytelling strategy with storytelling frameworks, story collection methods, and multimedia storytelling elements.

Prompt: As a Content Strategist, create a brand storytelling strategy for a nonprofit organization. The goal is to communicate the organization's mission, impact, and stories to connect with the audience and inspire action. Please highlight real-life stories, maintain authenticity, and adhere to the organization's values, using an emotional, compelling, and authentic style. Provide a created brand storytelling strategy with storytelling frameworks, story collection methods, and multimedia storytelling elements.

23.

[Role]: Content Strategist
[Task]: Develop a content marketing strategy for a new product launch.
[Context]: Creating a cohesive and impactful content plan to generate awareness and drive conversions.
[Goal]: Increase product visibility and engage the target audience.
[Constraints]: Limited resources and alignment with brand messaging.
[Style or Tone]: Strategic, data-driven, and aligned with the target audience.
[Structure or Format]: Prepared content marketing strategy document and key performance indicators (KPIs).

Prompt: As a Content Strategist, develop a content marketing strategy for a new product launch. The goal is to increase product visibility and engage the target audience. Please consider the limited resources and alignment with the brand messaging, using a strategic, data-driven, and audience-aligned style. Provide a prepared content marketing strategy document and key performance indicators (KPIs).

24.

[Role]: Content Strategist
[Task]: Create an email marketing content strategy for a B2C retail brand.
[Context]: The brand offers a wide range of products and aims to build customer loyalty and drive repeat purchases.
[Goal]: Deliver personalized and engaging email content to nurture

customer relationships, promote products, and boost sales.
[Constraints]: Segment the audience, automate email workflows, and comply with email marketing regulations.
[Style or Tone]: Personalized, persuasive, and visually appealing.
[Structure or Format]: Designed an email marketing content strategy with customer segmentation plans, email campaign templates, and performance tracking methods.

Prompt: As a Content Strategist, create an email marketing content strategy for a B2C retail brand. The goal is to deliver personalized and engaging email content to nurture customer relationships, promote products, and boost sales. Please segment the audience, automate email workflows, and comply with email marketing regulations, using a personalized, persuasive, and visually appealing style. Provide a designed email marketing content strategy with customer segmentation plans, email campaign templates, and performance tracking methods.

25.
[Role]: Content Strategist
[Task]: Develop a content strategy to align with business objectives.
[Context]: Planning and executing content initiatives.
[Goal]: Drive engagement, conversions, and brand consistency.
[Constraints]: Consider target audience, brand voice, and SEO best practices.
[Style or Tone]: Strategic, creative, and results-oriented.
[Structure or Format]: Prepared content strategy documents and implementation plans.

Prompt: As a Content Strategist, develop a content strategy to align with business objectives. The goal is to drive engagement, conversions, and brand consistency. Please consider the target audience, brand voice, and SEO best practices, using a strategic, creative, and results-oriented style. Provide prepared content strategy documents and implementation plans.

Prompts for Product Designers

1.

[Role]: Product Designer
[Task]: Create wireframes for a mobile application's onboarding screens.
[Context]: The onboarding screens aim to introduce users to the app's features.
[Goal]: Design intuitive and engaging onboarding experiences.
[Constraints]: Consider user flow, visual hierarchy, and interaction patterns.
[Style or Tone]: Clean, user-friendly, and visually appealing.
[Structure or Format]: Developed wireframes for onboarding screens, showcasing key screens and user interactions.

Prompt: As a Product Designer, create wireframes for a mobile application's onboarding screens. The goal is to design intuitive and engaging onboarding experiences. Please consider user flow, visual hierarchy, and interaction patterns, using a clean, user-friendly, and visually appealing style. Provide developed wireframes for onboarding screens, showcasing key screens and user interactions.

2.

[Role]: Product Designer
[Task]: Conduct user research to gather insights for a new product design.
[Context]: The goal is to understand user needs and preferences.
[Goal]: Gather qualitative and quantitative data to inform the product design process.
[Constraints]: Conduct user interviews, surveys, and usability testing.
[Style or Tone]: Empathetic, inquisitive, and open-minded.
[Structure or Format]: Prepared a research plan with objectives, methodology, and participant profiles.

Prompt: As a Product Designer, conduct user research to gather insights for a new product design. The goal is to gather qualitative and quantitative data to inform the product design process. Please conduct user interviews, surveys, and usability testing, using an empathetic, inquisitive, and open-minded approach. Provide a prepared research plan with objectives, methodology, and participant profiles.

3.

[Role]: Product Designer
[Task]: Conduct a competitive analysis of similar products in the market.
[Context]: Understanding the competitive landscape and identifying unique selling points.
[Goal]: Inform product differentiation and identify opportunities for improvement.
[Constraints]: Evaluate features, user experience, and visual design of competitor products.
[Style or Tone]: Analytical, comparative, and strategic.
[Structure or Format]: Prepared a competitive analysis report, highlighting key findings and recommendations.

Prompt: As a Product Designer, conduct a competitive analysis of similar products in the market. The goal is to inform product differentiation and identify opportunities for improvement. Please evaluate features, user experience, and visual design of competitor products, using an analytical, comparative, and strategic style. Provide a prepared competitive analysis report, highlighting key findings and recommendations.

4.

[Role]: Product Designer
[Task]: Design a user flow for a checkout process in an e-commerce app.
[Context]: Optimizing the checkout experience to maximize conversions.
[Goal]: Create a seamless and intuitive checkout journey.

[Constraints]: Consider input fields, payment options, and order confirmation.
[Style or Tone]: Simplified, efficient, and trustworthy.
[Structure or Format]: Created a user flow diagram for the checkout process, illustrating each step and decision point.

Prompt: As a Product Designer, design a user flow for a checkout process in an e-commerce app. The goal is to create a seamless and intuitive checkout journey. Please consider input fields, payment options, and order confirmation, using a simplified, efficient, and trustworthy style. Provide a created user flow diagram for the checkout process, illustrating each step and decision point.

5.
[Role]: Product Designer
[Task]: Select or create icons and images that effectively communicate meaning and enhance the user experience. Choose appropriate fonts and typography styles that are legible, accessible, and align with the overall design aesthetic.
[Context]: Enhancing the visual appeal and usability of the product design.
[Goal]: Create a cohesive and visually appealing user interface that effectively communicates information.
[Constraints]: Limited resources, consideration of brand guidelines, accessibility standards, and platform limitations.
[Style or Tone]: Creative, detail-oriented, and user-focused.
[Structure or Format]: Develop a style guide that includes guidelines for iconography, imagery, and typography choices, along with practical examples and implementation considerations.

Prompt: As a Product Designer, your role includes selecting or creating icons and images that effectively communicate meaning and enhance the user experience. Additionally, you need to choose appropriate fonts and typography styles that are legible, accessible, and align with the overall design aesthetic. The goal is to create a cohesive and visually appealing user interface that effectively communicates information. Develop a style guide that includes guidelines for iconography, imagery, and typography choices. Please consider the limited resources, brand guidelines, accessibility standards, and platform limitations. Include practical examples and implementation considerations in the style guide to ensure consistent and successful application of iconography, imagery, and typography throughout the product design.

6.

[Role]: Product Designer
[Task]: Conduct user testing sessions to gather feedback on a new product prototype.
[Context]: The goal is to validate the usability and effectiveness of the design.
[Goal]: Identify usability issues and gather insights for iterative improvements.
[Constraints]: Create test scenarios, facilitate user sessions, and capture feedback.
[Style or Tone]: Empathetic, observant, and non-directive.
[Structure or Format]: Compiled a user testing report with participant feedback, observations, and recommendations.

Prompt: As a Product Designer, conduct user testing sessions to gather feedback on a new product prototype. The goal is to identify usability issues and gather insights for iterative improvements. Please create test scenarios, facilitate user sessions, and capture feedback, using an empathetic, observant, and non-directive style. Provide a compiled user testing report with participant feedback, observations, and recommendations.

7.

[Role]: Product Designer
[Task]: Create user stories to effectively communicate and capture user needs and requirements.
[Context]: Enhancing the product development process by aligning design decisions with user expectations.
[Goal]: Develop a structured approach to crafting user stories that accurately reflect user needs and enable efficient product design.
[Constraints]: Limited time for user research and story creation, consideration of budget constraints.
[Style or Tone]: Clear, concise, and user-centric.
[Structure or Format]: Develop a user story template and utilize user research methods to gather insights for effective story creation.

Prompt: As a Product Designer, it is my responsibility to create user stories that effectively capture user needs and requirements. This ensures that design decisions align with user expectations, ultimately enhancing the product development process. Develop a structured approach to crafting user stories within the given time constraints, while considering budget limitations. Maintain a clear, concise, and user-centric style and utilize user research methods to gather insights for accurate story creation.

8.

[Role]: Product Designer
[Task]: Design intuitive and visually appealing user interfaces.
[Context]: Creating engaging and delightful user experiences.
[Goal]: Enhance usability and user satisfaction.
[Constraints]: Apply design principles and best practices.
[Style or Tone]: Creative, user-centered, and aesthetically pleasing.
[Structure or Format]: Prepared UI mockups or prototypes, showcasing the interface design.

Prompt: As a Product Designer, design intuitive and visually appealing user interfaces. The goal is to enhance usability and user satisfaction. Please apply design principles and best practices, using a creative, user-centered, and aesthetically pleasing style. Provide prepared UI mockups or prototypes, showcasing the interface design.

9.

[Role]: Product Designer
[Task]: Stay updated with the latest design trends, emerging technologies, and industry best practices.
[Context]: Enhancing the ability to deliver innovative and competitive product designs.
[Goal]: Continuously improve design skills and knowledge to create cutting-edge products.
[Constraints]: Limited time for learning and implementation, consideration of budget constraints.
[Style or Tone]: Proactive, research-driven, and forward-thinking.
[Structure or Format]: Develop a personalized learning plan that includes resources, workshops, and activities to stay updated with design trends, emerging technologies, and industry best practices.

Prompt: As a Product Designer, it is essential to stay updated with the latest design trends, emerging technologies, and industry best practices. This helps in delivering innovative and competitive product designs. Develop a personalized learning plan that includes resources, workshops, and activities to stay updated within the limited time available. Please consider any budget constraints and focus on a proactive, research-driven approach to continuously improve your design skills and knowledge, ensuring you can create cutting-edge products.

10.

[Role]: Product Designer
[Task]: Conduct user research to understand target users' needs and pain points.
[Context]: Informing the design process with user-centered insights.
[Goal]: Identify user requirements and inform product decisions.
[Constraints]: Plan and conduct user interviews, surveys, and usability tests.
[Style or Tone]: Empathetic, inquisitive, and open-minded.
[Structure or Format]: Prepared a user research report, summarizing key findings and actionable recommendations.

Prompt: As a Product Designer, conduct user research to understand target users' needs and pain points. The goal is to identify user requirements and inform product decisions. Please plan and conduct user interviews, surveys, and usability tests, using an empathetic, inquisitive, and open-minded style. Provide a prepared user research report, summarizing key findings and actionable recommendations.

11.

[Role]: Product Designer
[Task]: Collaborate with developers to ensure the implementation of design specifications.
[Context]: Bridging the gap between design and development teams.
[Goal]: Maintain design integrity and achieve a high-quality user experience.
[Constraints]: Provide design assets, guidelines, and clarifications to developers.
[Style or Tone]: Collaborative, communicative, and detail-oriented.
[Structure or Format]: Prepared design specification documents, detailing UI requirements and interactions.

Prompt: As a Product Designer, collaborate with developers to ensure the implementation of design specifications. The goal is to maintain design integrity and achieve a high-quality user experience. Please provide design assets, guidelines, and clarifications to developers, using a collaborative, communicative, and detail-oriented style. Provide prepared design specification documents, detailing UI requirements and interactions.

12.

[Role]: Product Designer
[Task]: Conduct A/B testing to compare the performance of design variations.
[Context]: Optimizing design decisions based on data-driven insights.
[Goal]: Identify the most effective design solution.
[Constraints]: Define hypotheses, design and implement A/B tests, analyze and interpret results.
[Style or Tone]: Data-driven, objective, and iterative.
[Structure or Format]: Prepared an A/B testing report, summarizing findings and recommendations.

Prompt: As a Product Designer, conduct A/B testing to compare the performance of design variations. The goal is to identify the most effective design solution. Please define hypotheses, design and implement A/B tests, analyze and interpret results, using a data-driven, objective, and iterative style. Provide a prepared A/B testing report, summarizing findings and recommendations.

13.

[Role]: Product Designer
[Task]: Design a user interface for a mobile app's settings screen.
[Context]: Optimizing the settings screen for simplicity and ease of use.
[Goal]: Create a clear and organized layout for accessing app preferences.
[Constraints]: Consider user preferences, accessibility, and visual hierarchy.

[Style or Tone]: Clean, minimalist, and intuitive.
[Structure or Format]: Developed UI mockups for the settings screen, showcasing layout and visual elements.

Prompt: As a Product Designer, design a user interface for a mobile app's settings screen. The goal is to create a clear and organized layout for accessing app preferences. Please consider user preferences, accessibility, and visual hierarchy, using a clean, minimalist, and intuitive style. Provide developed UI mockups for the settings screen, showcasing layout and visual elements.

14.
[Role]: Product Designer
[Task]: Conduct a heuristic evaluation of a website's mobile user interface.
[Context]: Identifying mobile-specific usability issues and design improvements.
[Goal]: Provide actionable recommendations to enhance mobile user experience.
[Constraints]: Evaluate responsiveness, touch interactions, and mobile-specific elements.
[Style or Tone]: Critical, detail-oriented, and platform-specific.
[Structure or Format]: Prepared a heuristic evaluation report focused on mobile interface, highlighting findings and suggested improvements.

Prompt: As a Product Designer, conduct a heuristic evaluation of a website's mobile user interface. The goal is to provide actionable recommendations to enhance mobile user experience. Please evaluate responsiveness, touch interactions, and mobile-specific elements, using a critical, detail-oriented, and platform-specific style. Provide a prepared heuristic evaluation report focused on the mobile interface, highlighting findings and suggested improvements.

15.

[Role]: Product Designer
[Task]: Collaborate with the development team to create wireframes for a responsive web application.
[Context]: Designing a user-friendly and visually cohesive interface across different screen sizes.
[Goal]: Ensure consistent user experience and seamless navigation.
[Constraints]: Limited development resources, consideration of performance and loading time.
[Style or Tone]: Collaborative, iterative, and visual.
[Structure or Format]: Create wireframes showcasing the main interface elements, navigation patterns, and responsive design considerations.

Prompt: As a Product Designer, collaborate with the development team to create wireframes for a responsive web application. The goal is to ensure a consistent user experience and seamless navigation across different screen sizes. Please consider the limited development resources and the need to optimize performance and loading time. Create wireframes showcasing the main interface elements, navigation patterns, and responsive design considerations.

16.

[Role]: Product Designer
[Task]: Collaborate with the development team to define user stories and acceptance criteria.
[Context]: Aligning design and development efforts for efficient product delivery.
[Goal]: Create a shared understanding and clear expectations for feature implementation.
[Constraints]: Define user stories, acceptance criteria, and collaborate with the development team.
[Style or Tone]: Collaborative, concise, and actionable.

[Structure or Format]: Developed user stories and acceptance criteria documents for the development team.

Prompt: As a Product Designer, collaborate with the development team to define user stories and acceptance criteria. The goal is to create a shared understanding and clear expectations for feature implementation. Please define user stories, acceptance criteria, and collaborate with the development team, using a collaborative, concise, and actionable style. Provide developed user stories and acceptance criteria documents for the development team.

17.

[Role]: Product Designer
[Task]: Conduct a usability review of a mobile app's navigation structure.
[Context]: Evaluating the effectiveness and efficiency of app navigation.
[Goal]: Identify navigation issues and propose improvements for seamless user flow.
[Constraints]: Evaluate navigation patterns, information hierarchy, and user feedback.
[Style or Tone]: Objective, detailed, and user-centric.
[Structure or Format]: Prepared a usability review report, outlining navigation findings and suggested enhancements.

Prompt: As a Product Designer, conduct a usability review of a mobile app's navigation structure. The goal is to identify navigation issues and propose improvements for seamless user flow. Please evaluate navigation patterns, information hierarchy, and user feedback, using an objective, detailed, and user-centric style. Provide a prepared usability review report, outlining navigation findings and suggested enhancements.

18.

[Role]: Product Designer
[Task]: Design a user interface for a web-based dashboard.

[Context]: Creating a visually appealing and intuitive data visualization platform.
[Goal]: Enable users to easily access and understand complex data.
[Constraints]: Consider data presentation, interaction patterns, and responsive design.
[Style or Tone]: Modern, data-driven, and intuitive.
[Structure or Format]: Developed UI mockups for the web-based dashboard, showcasing data visualization and interaction elements.

Prompt: As a Product Designer, design a user interface for a web-based dashboard. The goal is to enable users to easily access and understand complex data. Please consider data presentation, interaction patterns, and responsive design, using a modern, data-driven, and intuitive style. Provide developed UI mockups for the web-based dashboard, showcasing data visualization and interaction elements.

19.
[Role]: Product Designer
[Task]: Mentoring junior designers
[Context]: Sharing knowledge, providing guidance, and supporting the growth of junior designers in their career development.
[Goal]: Foster a collaborative and supportive design culture, enhance the skills and confidence of junior designers, and elevate the overall design team's capabilities.
[Constraints]: Limited time and resources, balancing mentoring responsibilities with project deadlines.
[Style or Tone]: Supportive, collaborative, and constructive.
[Structure or Format]: Conducting regular one-on-one mentoring sessions, providing feedback on design work, sharing resources and industry insights.

Prompt: As a Product Designer, mentoring junior designers is an essential aspect of your role in nurturing the next generation of design talent. Schedule regular one-on-one mentoring sessions to create a safe space for junior designers to ask questions, seek guidance, and share their design challenges. Provide constructive feedback on their design work, highlighting areas of improvement and celebrating their successes. Share resources, industry insights, and best practices to help them expand their design knowledge and skills. Encourage collaboration and create opportunities for junior designers to work on challenging projects that foster growth and development. Your goal is to cultivate a collaborative and supportive design culture, where junior designers feel empowered, confident, and inspired to contribute their best work.

20.

[Role]: Product Designer
[Task]: Create wireframes and interactive prototypes for a mobile app.
[Context]: Translating conceptual ideas into tangible user interface designs.
[Goal]: Visualize and validate the app's user flow and interactions.
[Constraints]: Use wireframing tools to create low-fidelity prototypes.
[Style or Tone]: Clean, intuitive, and interactive.
[Structure or Format]: Prepared wireframes and interactive prototypes, showcasing app screens and user interactions.

Prompt: As a Product Designer, create wireframes and interactive prototypes for a mobile app. The goal is to visualize and validate the app's user flow and interactions. Please use wireframing tools to create low-fidelity prototypes, using a clean, intuitive, and interactive style. Provide prepared wireframes and interactive prototypes, showcasing app screens and user interactions.

21.

[Role]: Product Designer
[Task]: Conduct a design review of an existing product's user interface.

[Context]: Evaluating the usability and visual appeal of the interface.
[Goal]: Identify design flaws and propose enhancements for better user experience.
[Constraints]: Evaluate information layout, visual hierarchy, and consistency.
[Style or Tone]: Objective, constructive, and detail-oriented.
[Structure or Format]: Prepared a design review report, highlighting usability findings and suggested improvements.

Prompt: As a Product Designer, conduct a design review of an existing product's user interface. The goal is to identify design flaws and propose enhancements for better user experience. Please evaluate information layout, visual hierarchy, and consistency, using an objective, constructive, and detail-oriented style. Provide a prepared design review report, highlighting usability findings and suggested improvements.

22.
[Role]: Product Designer
[Task]: Collaborate with stakeholders to define product requirements and goals.
[Context]: Aligning business objectives with user needs.
[Goal]: Establish a shared vision and clear direction for the product.
[Constraints]: Conduct stakeholder interviews and facilitate workshops.
[Style or Tone]: Collaborative, communicative, and goal-oriented.
[Structure or Format]: Prepared a product requirements document, outlining goals, features, and success criteria.

Prompt: As a Product Designer, collaborate with stakeholders to define product requirements and goals. The goal is to establish a shared vision and clear direction for the product. Please conduct stakeholder interviews and facilitate workshops, using a collaborative, communicative, and goal-oriented style. Provide a prepared product requirements document, outlining goals, features, and success criteria.

23.

[Role]: Product Designer
[Task]: Conduct user research to understand user behavior and preferences.
[Context]: Informing design decisions based on user insights.
[Goal]: Identify user needs and design solutions that meet their requirements.
[Constraints]: Plan and conduct user interviews, surveys, and usability tests.
[Style or Tone]: Empathetic, curious, and open-minded.
[Structure or Format]: Prepared a user research report, summarizing key findings and actionable recommendations.

Prompt: As a Product Designer, conduct user research to understand user behavior and preferences. The goal is to identify user needs and design solutions that meet their requirements. Please plan and conduct user interviews, surveys, and usability tests, using an empathetic, curious, and open-minded style. Provide a prepared user research report, summarizing key findings and actionable recommendations.

24.

[Role]: Product Designer
[Task]: Create wireframes and interactive prototypes for a web application.
[Context]: Translating design concepts into tangible user interface designs.
[Goal]: Visualize and validate the web application's user flow and interactions.
[Constraints]: Use wireframing tools to create low-fidelity prototypes.
[Style or Tone]: Clean, intuitive, and interactive.
[Structure or Format]: Prepared wireframes and interactive prototypes, showcasing web application screens and user interactions.

Prompt: As a Product Designer, create wireframes and interactive prototypes for a web application. The goal is to visualize and validate the web application's user flow and interactions. Please use wireframing tools to create low-fidelity prototypes, using a clean, intuitive, and interactive style. Provide prepared wireframes and interactive prototypes, showcasing web application screens and user interactions.

25.

[Role]: Product Designer
[Task]: Conduct a usability evaluation of an existing mobile app.
[Context]: Assessing the app's usability and identifying areas for improvement.
[Goal]: Identify usability issues and propose enhancements for a better user experience.
[Constraints]: Evaluate navigation, layout, and interaction patterns.
[Style or Tone]: Objective, detailed, and user-centric.
[Structure or Format]: Prepared a usability evaluation report, outlining findings and recommended improvements.

Prompt: As a Product Designer, conduct a usability evaluation of an existing mobile app. The goal is to identify usability issues and propose enhancements for a better user experience. Please evaluate navigation, layout, and interaction patterns, using an objective, detailed, and user-centric style. Provide a prepared usability evaluation report, outlining findings and recommended improvements.

Prompts for UX Researchers

1.

[Role]: UX Researcher
[Task]: Conduct user interviews to gather insights and understand user needs.
[Context]: Informing the design process with user-centered perspectives.
[Goal]: Identify user pain points and opportunities for improvement.
[Constraints]: Plan and conduct structured interviews, probe for deep insights.

[Style or Tone]: Empathetic, open-minded, and non-directive.
[Structure or Format]: Prepared interview guides and transcripts, capturing key insights.

Prompt: As a UX Researcher, conduct user interviews to gather insights and understand user needs. The goal is to identify user pain points and opportunities for improvement. Please plan and conduct structured interviews, probe for deep insights, using an empathetic, open-minded, and non-directive style. Provide prepared interview guides and transcripts, capturing key insights.

2.
[Role]: UX Researcher
[Task]: Conduct a diary study to gather longitudinal insights into users' experiences with a fitness tracking app.
[Context]: Understanding user behavior and uncovering patterns over time.
[Goal]: Gain in-depth understanding of user engagement and pain points with the fitness tracking app.
[Constraints]: Participants' time commitment, need for consistent data collection methods.
[Style or Tone]: Empathetic, reflective, and qualitative.
[Structure or Format]: Prepared diary study guidelines with sections for participant instructions, data collection templates, and reflection prompts.

Prompt: As a UX Researcher, conduct a diary study to gather longitudinal insights into users' experiences with a fitness tracking app. The goal is to gain an in-depth understanding of user engagement and pain points with the app. Please consider the participants' time commitment and the need for consistent data collection methods. Provide prepared diary study guidelines with sections for participant instructions, data collection templates, and reflection prompts.

3.

[Role]: UX Researcher
[Task]: Plan and conduct usability tests to evaluate product usability.
[Context]: Identifying usability issues and areas for improvement.
[Goal]: Provide actionable recommendations for enhancing user experience.
[Constraints]: Develop test scenarios, observe user interactions, and collect feedback.
[Style or Tone]: Observational, detail-oriented, and user-centric.
[Structure or Format]: Prepared usability testing plans and reports, highlighting findings.

Prompt: As a UX Researcher, plan and conduct usability tests to evaluate product usability. The goal is to provide actionable recommendations for enhancing user experience. Please develop test scenarios, observe user interactions, and collect feedback, using an observational, detail-oriented, and user-centric style. Provide prepared usability testing plans and reports, highlighting findings.

4.

[Role]: UX Researcher
[Task]: Conduct competitive analysis to understand market trends and benchmark products.
[Context]: Assessing the strengths and weaknesses of competing solutions.
[Goal]: Identify opportunities for differentiation and improvement.
[Constraints]: Analyze competitor websites, apps, and marketing materials.
[Style or Tone]: Analytical, comparative, and strategic.
[Structure or Format]: Prepared competitive analysis reports, outlining key findings.

Prompt: As a UX Researcher, conduct competitive analysis to understand market trends and benchmark products. The goal is to identify opportunities for differentiation and improvement. Please analyze competitor websites, apps, and marketing materials, using an analytical, comparative, and strategic style. Provide prepared competitive analysis reports, outlining key findings.

5.

[Role]: UX Researcher
[Task]: Conduct card sorting exercises to inform information architecture.
[Context]: Organizing and structuring content for optimal user navigation.
[Goal]: Determine intuitive information groupings and labeling.
[Constraints]: Plan and conduct card sorting sessions, analyze results.
[Style or Tone]: Structured, systematic, and user-centered.
[Structure or Format]: Prepared card sorting protocols and analysis summaries.

Prompt: As a UX Researcher, conduct card sorting exercises to inform information architecture. The goal is to determine intuitive information groupings and labeling. Please plan and conduct card sorting sessions, analyze results, using a structured, systematic, and user-centered style. Provide prepared card sorting protocols and analysis summaries.

6.

[Role]: UX Researcher
[Task]: Conduct user surveys to collect quantitative feedback on product features.
[Context]: Gathering data to support evidence-based decision-making.
[Goal]: Identify feature preferences and prioritize development efforts.
[Constraints]: Design and distribute surveys, analyze and interpret survey data.
[Style or Tone]: Objective, concise, and actionable.
[Structure or Format]: Prepared survey questionnaires and analysis reports.

Prompt: As a UX Researcher, conduct user surveys to collect quantitative feedback on product features. The goal is to identify feature preferences and prioritize development efforts. Please design and distribute surveys, analyze and interpret survey data, using an objective, concise, and actionable style. Provide prepared survey questionnaires and analysis reports.

7.

[Role]: UX Researcher
[Task]: Conduct ethnographic research to gain deep insights into user behaviors.
[Context]: Understanding the cultural and social context of user experiences.
[Goal]: Uncover user needs, motivations, and pain points.
[Constraints]: Conduct field observations, interviews, and cultural probes.
[Style or Tone]: Immersive, empathetic, and reflective.
[Structure or Format]: Prepared ethnographic research reports, presenting rich user narratives.

Prompt: As a UX Researcher, conduct ethnographic research to gain deep insights into user behaviors. The goal is to uncover user needs, motivations, and pain points. Please conduct field observations, interviews, and cultural probes, using an immersive, empathetic, and reflective style. Provide prepared ethnographic research reports, presenting rich user narratives.

8.

[Role]: UX Researcher
[Task]: Facilitate design workshops to generate ideas and foster collaboration.
[Context]: Engaging cross-functional teams in the design process.
[Goal]: Generate innovative design concepts and gather diverse perspectives.
[Constraints]: Plan and lead workshops, encourage active participation.
[Style or Tone]: Creative, inclusive, and facilitative.
[Structure or Format]: Prepared workshop agendas and documentation of outcomes.

Prompt: As a UX Researcher, facilitate design workshops to generate ideas and foster collaboration. The goal is to generate innovative design concepts and gather diverse perspectives. Please plan and lead workshops, encourage active participation, using a creative, inclusive, and facilitative style. Provide prepared workshop agendas and documentation of outcomes.

9.
[Role]: UX Researcher
[Task]: Conduct user journey mapping exercises to visualize and analyze user experiences.
[Context]: Understanding the end-to-end user journey and identifying pain points.
[Goal]: Identify opportunities for improving the user experience.
[Constraints]: Facilitate collaborative mapping sessions, gather user insights.
[Style or Tone]: Visual, holistic, and empathetic.
[Structure or Format]: Prepared user journey maps in table form, highlighting key touchpoints.

Prompt: As a UX Researcher, conduct user journey mapping exercises to visualize and analyze user experiences. The goal is to identify opportunities for improving the user experience. Please facilitate collaborative mapping sessions, gather user insights, using a visual, holistic, and empathetic style. Provide prepared user journey maps in table form, highlighting key touchpoints.

10.
[Role]: UX Researcher
[Task]: Familiarize yourself with various testing methods and their best-suited scenarios to gather data for making informed design decisions.
[Context]: Enhancing the ability to gather relevant data and make data-driven design solutions.

[Goal]: Understand the different testing methods available and their applications to ensure informed decision-making in design solutions.
[Constraints]: Limited time and resources, consideration of participant availability and diversity.
[Style or Tone]: Informative, research-oriented, and analytical.
[Structure or Format]: Create a comprehensive guide that outlines different testing methods, their purposes, advantages, and ideal scenarios for implementation.

Prompt: As a UX Researcher, it is important to be familiar with various testing methods and their best-suited scenarios to gather data that enables informed design decisions. Develop a comprehensive guide that outlines different testing methods, including usability testing, A/B testing, eye tracking, interviews, surveys, and more. For each testing method, describe its purpose, advantages, and the specific scenarios where it is most effective. Consider the constraints of limited time and resources, as well as the availability and diversity of participants. Your goal is to provide a valuable resource that helps the team understand and choose the most appropriate testing methods for gathering relevant data and making data-driven design solutions.

11.

[Role]: UX Researcher
[Task]: Create user personas to represent target audience segments.
[Context]: Developing a shared understanding of user needs and behaviors.
[Goal]: Inform design decisions and promote user empathy.
[Constraints]: Conduct user research, analyze data, and create profiles.
[Style or Tone]: Empathetic, descriptive, and relatable.
[Structure or Format]: Prepared user persona profiles, including key characteristics.

Prompt: As a UX Researcher, create user personas to represent target audience segments. The goal is to inform design decisions and promote user empathy. Please conduct user research, analyze data, and create profiles, using an empathetic, descriptive, and relatable style. Provide prepared user persona profiles, including key characteristics.

12.

[Role]: UX Researcher
[Task]: Conduct heuristic evaluations to identify usability issues in products.
[Context]: Evaluating user interfaces against established usability principles.
[Goal]: Provide actionable recommendations for improving usability.
[Constraints]: Assess user interfaces, identify usability violations.
[Style or Tone]: Critical, systematic, and evaluative.
[Structure or Format]: Prepared heuristic evaluation reports, highlighting findings.

Prompt: As a UX Researcher, conduct heuristic evaluations to identify usability issues in products. The goal is to provide actionable recommendations for improving usability. Please assess user interfaces, identify usability violations, using a critical, systematic, and evaluative style. Provide prepared heuristic evaluation reports, highlighting findings.

13.

[Role]: UX Researcher
[Task]: Conduct usability testing sessions to evaluate the user experience of a product.
[Context]: Assessing the effectiveness, efficiency, and satisfaction of interactions.
[Goal]: Identify usability issues and gather user feedback for improvements.
[Constraints]: Plan and conduct usability tests, analyze and report findings.
[Style or Tone]: User-centric, interactive, and informative.
[Structure or Format]: Prepared usability test scripts and detailed test reports.

Prompt: As a UX Researcher, conduct usability testing sessions to evaluate the user experience of a product. The goal is to identify usability issues and gather user feedback for improvements. Please plan and conduct usability tests, analyze and report findings, using a user-centric, interactive, and informative style. Provide prepared usability test scripts and detailed test reports.

14.

[Role]: UX Researcher
[Task]: Conduct user interviews to gather qualitative insights and user feedback.
[Context]: Understanding user needs, goals, and pain points.
[Goal]: Uncover user motivations and inform design decisions.
[Constraints]: Plan and conduct interviews, capture and analyze interview data.
[Style or Tone]: Inquisitive, conversational, and empathetic.
[Structure or Format]: Prepared interview guides and detailed interview summaries.

Prompt: As a UX Researcher, conduct user interviews to gather qualitative insights and user feedback. The goal is to uncover user motivations and inform design decisions. Please plan and conduct interviews, capture and analyze interview data, using an inquisitive, conversational, and empathetic style. Provide prepared interview guides and detailed interview summaries.

15.

[Role]: UX Researcher
[Task]: Analyze user analytics data to gain insights into user behavior.
[Context]: Leveraging data to understand user engagement and usage patterns.
[Goal]: Identify trends and opportunities for optimization.
[Constraints]: Analyze user data, generate actionable recommendations.

[Style or Tone]: Analytical, data-driven, and insightful.
[Structure or Format]: Prepared data analysis reports and visualization.

Prompt: As a UX Researcher, analyze user analytics data to gain insights into user behavior. The goal is to identify trends and opportunities for optimization. Please analyze user data, generate actionable recommendations, using an analytical, data-driven, and insightful style. Provide prepared data analysis reports and visualizations.

16.
[Role]: UX Researcher
[Task]: Conduct a contextual inquiry to understand the workflow and pain points of healthcare professionals using a medical software.
[Context]: Improving the user experience and efficiency of the medical software.
[Goal]: Identify usability issues and gather insights for redesigning the software.
[Constraints]: Limited access to healthcare professionals' schedules, need for confidentiality of patient information.
[Style or Tone]: Empathetic, inquisitive, and professional.
[Structure or Format]: Prepared contextual inquiry guide with sections for interview questions, observation guidelines, and data analysis.

Prompt: As a UX Researcher, conduct a contextual inquiry to understand the workflow and pain points of healthcare professionals using a medical software. The goal is to identify usability issues and gather insights for redesigning the software. Please consider the limited access to healthcare professionals' schedules and the need for confidentiality of patient information. Provide a prepared contextual inquiry guide with sections for interview questions, observation guidelines, and data analysis.

17.

[Role]: UX Researcher
[Task]: Analyze quantitative data from an online survey to understand user satisfaction with a mobile banking app.
[Context]: Assessing the app's performance and identifying areas for improvement.
[Goal]: Extract meaningful insights from the survey data and make data-driven recommendations.
[Constraints]: Large dataset to analyze, need for statistical analysis techniques.
[Style or Tone]: Analytical, precise, and evidence-based.
[Structure or Format]: Prepared survey data analysis plan with sections for data cleaning, statistical analysis, and result interpretation.

Prompt: As a UX Researcher, analyze quantitative data from an online survey to understand user satisfaction with a mobile banking app. The goal is to extract meaningful insights from the survey data and make data-driven recommendations. Please consider the large dataset to analyze and the need for statistical analysis techniques. Provide a prepared survey data analysis plan with sections for data cleaning, statistical analysis, and result interpretation.

18.

[Role]: UX Researcher
[Task]: Collaborate with cross-functional teams to define user research goals.
[Context]: Aligning research objectives with product and business goals.
[Goal]: Establish a shared understanding and focus for research efforts.
[Constraints]: Engage with stakeholders, gather requirements, and prioritize goals.
[Style or Tone]: Collaborative, goal-oriented, and inclusive.
[Structure or Format]: Prepared research goal statements and project briefs.

Prompt: As a UX Researcher, collaborate with cross-functional teams to define user research goals. The goal is to establish a shared understanding and focus for research efforts. Please engage with stakeholders, gather requirements, and prioritize goals, using a collaborative, goal-oriented, and inclusive style. Provide prepared research goal statements and project briefs.

19.

[Role]: UX Researcher
[Task]: Synthesize research findings into actionable insights and recommendations.
[Context]: Analyzing and distilling data from various research methods.
[Goal]: Communicate research findings in a concise and impactful manner.
[Constraints]: Analyze research data, identify patterns, and draw meaningful conclusions.
[Style or Tone]: Clear, concise, and persuasive.
[Structure or Format]: Prepared research insights reports and presentation slides.

Prompt: As a UX Researcher, synthesize research findings into actionable insights and recommendations. The goal is to communicate research findings in a concise and impactful manner. Please analyze research data, identify patterns, and draw meaningful conclusions, using a clear, concise, and persuasive style. Provide prepared research insights reports and presentation slides.

20.

[Role]: UX Researcher
[Task]: Conduct an expert review of a website's navigation structure.
[Context]: Evaluating the website's ease of use and findability.
[Goal]: Identify navigation design flaws and provide recommendations for improvement.

[Constraints]: Limited time for the review, need for thorough evaluation.
[Style or Tone]: Analytical, objective, and actionable.
[Structure or Format]: Prepared expert review checklist with sections for navigation elements, findings, and recommendations.

Prompt: As a UX Researcher, conduct an expert review of a website's navigation structure. The goal is to identify navigation design flaws and provide recommendations for improvement. Please consider the limited time for the review and the need for a thorough evaluation. Provide a prepared expert review checklist with sections for navigation elements, findings, and recommendations.

21.
[Role]: UX Researcher
[Task]: Conduct user interviews to gather feedback on a mobile app's user interface.
[Context]: Evaluating the usability and effectiveness of the app's design.
[Goal]: Identify areas for improvement and gather insights for future iterations.
[Constraints]: Limited time for each interview and need for unbiased feedback.
[Style or Tone]: Open-ended, conversational, and non-leading.
[Structure or Format]: Prepared interview script with sections for introductory questions, task scenarios, and follow-up probes.

Prompt: As a UX Researcher, conduct user interviews to gather feedback on a mobile app's user interface. The goal is to identify areas for improvement and gather insights for future iterations. Please consider the limited time for each interview and the need for unbiased feedback. Provide a prepared interview script with sections for introductory questions, task scenarios, and follow-up probes.

22.

[Role]: UX Researcher
[Task]: Design and administer an online survey to gather user preferences for a website's layout.
[Context]: Understanding user preferences and optimizing the website's design.
[Goal]: Obtain quantitative data to inform design decisions.
[Constraints]: Limited survey length and need for clear and focused questions.
[Style or Tone]: Clear, concise, and easily understandable.
[Structure or Format]: Prepared survey template with sections for demographic questions, likert-scale ratings, and open-ended comments.

Prompt: As a UX Researcher, design and administer an online survey to gather user preferences for a website's layout. The goal is to obtain quantitative data to inform design decisions. Please consider the limited survey length and the need for clear and focused questions. Provide a prepared survey template with sections for demographic questions, likert-scale ratings, and open-ended comments.

23.

[Role]: UX Researcher
[Task]: Conduct an ethnographic study to observe and document user behavior in a retail environment.
[Context]: Understanding user needs, preferences, and pain points.
[Goal]: Identify opportunities for improving the retail experience.
[Constraints]: Limited observation time and need for non-intrusive data collection.
[Style or Tone]: Detailed, observational, and objective.
[Structure or Format]: Prepared observation checklist with sections for user behaviors, environmental factors, and key observations.

Prompt: As a UX Researcher, conduct an ethnographic study to observe and document user behavior in a retail environment. The goal is to identify opportunities for improving the retail experience. Please consider the limited observation time and the need for non-intrusive data collection. Provide a prepared observation checklist with sections for user behaviors, environmental factors, and key observations.

24.

[Role]: UX Researcher

[Task]: Facilitate a focus group discussion to gather insights on a new software feature.

[Context]: Exploring user perceptions, preferences, and expectations.

[Goal]: Obtain qualitative data to inform feature development and refinement.

[Constraints]: Limited time for the focus group and need for balanced participation.

[Style or Tone]: Facilitative, inclusive, and unbiased.

[Structure or Format]: Prepared focus group discussion guide with sections for introduction, topic exploration, and closing remarks.

Prompt: As a UX Researcher, facilitate a focus group discussion to gather insights on a new software feature. The goal is to obtain qualitative data to inform feature development and refinement. Please consider the limited time for the focus group and the need for balanced participation. Provide a prepared focus group discussion guide with sections for introduction, topic exploration, and closing remarks.

25.

[Role]: UX Researcher

[Task]: Generate relevant and effective questions for a user survey that gather insightful data for user research purposes.

[Context]: Conducting user surveys to gather quantitative and qualitative

data for understanding user behaviors, preferences, and needs.
[Goal]: Develop a well-crafted survey questionnaire that captures valuable insights and helps inform design decisions.
[Constraints]: Consideration of survey length, clarity of questions, avoiding bias, and ensuring data reliability.
[Style or Tone]: Clear, concise, and neutral.
[Structure or Format]: Create a user survey question bank that includes various question types, such as multiple-choice, rating scales, and open-ended questions. Provide guidelines for question formulation, examples of effective questions, and considerations for survey flow.

Prompt: As a UX Researcher, your responsibility is to generate relevant and effective questions for a user survey that gather insightful data for user research purposes. Develop a comprehensive user survey question bank that covers a range of topics related to user behaviors, preferences, and needs. Consider the goals of the research and the specific insights you aim to gather. Ensure the questions are clear, concise, and neutral, avoiding any potential bias. Include various question types, such as multiple-choice, rating scales, and open-ended questions, to capture different perspectives and levels of detail. Provide guidelines for formulating effective questions, examples of well-crafted survey questions, and considerations for survey flow and length. Your goal is to create a user survey questionnaire that captures valuable insights and helps inform design decisions based on reliable data.

Prompts for Documentation Writers

1.

[Role]: Documentation Writer
[Task]: Create a user manual for a software application.
[Context]: The software application has various features and functionalities.
[Goal]: Provide clear and comprehensive instructions to users on how to use the software effectively.

[Constraints]: Use screenshots, step-by-step instructions, and terminology that is easily understandable for the target audience.
[Style or Tone]: Informative, organized, and user-friendly.
[Structure or Format]: Created a user manual with chapters, sections, and visually appealing layout.

Prompt: As a Documentation Writer, create a user manual for a software application. The goal is to provide clear and comprehensive instructions to users on how to use the software effectively. Please use screenshots, step-by-step instructions, and terminology that is easily understandable for the target audience, using an informative, organized, and user-friendly style. Provide a created user manual with chapters, sections, and a visually appealing layout.

2.
[Role]: Documentation Writer
[Task]: Write release notes for a new software version.
[Context]: The software version includes bug fixes, feature enhancements, and known issues.
[Goal]: Communicate the changes and improvements to users in a concise and easily understandable manner.
[Constraints]: Use a standardized format, include version details, and highlight significant changes.
[Style or Tone]: Clear, concise, and professional.
[Structure or Format]: Prepared release notes with a section for each bug fix, feature enhancement, and known issue.

Prompt: As a Documentation Writer, write release notes for a new software version. The goal is to communicate the changes and improvements to users in a concise and easily understandable manner. Please use a standardized format, include version details, and highlight significant changes, using a clear, concise, and professional style. Provide prepared release notes with a section for each bug fix, feature enhancement, and known issue.

3.

[Role]: Documentation Writer
[Task]: Develop an API documentation for a web service.
[Context]: The web service provides various endpoints and functionalities for developers.
[Goal]: Provide developers with comprehensive information on how to integrate and utilize the web service's API.
[Constraints]: Use code samples, clear explanations, and endpoint descriptions.
[Style or Tone]: Technical, detailed, and developer-oriented.
[Structure or Format]: Developed API documentation with sections for each endpoint, parameters, response formats, and authentication.

Prompt: As a Documentation Writer, develop an API documentation for a web service. The goal is to provide developers with comprehensive information on how to integrate and utilize the web service's API. Please use code samples, clear explanations, and endpoint descriptions, using a technical, detailed, and developer-oriented style. Provide a developed API documentation with sections for each endpoint, parameters, response formats, and authentication.

4.

[Role]: Documentation Writer
[Task]: Create a troubleshooting guide for a software application.
[Context]: The software application may encounter common issues and errors.
[Goal]: Assist users in resolving problems and technical difficulties they may encounter.
[Constraints]: Provide step-by-step troubleshooting instructions, include relevant error messages, and suggest potential solutions.
[Style or Tone]: Problem-solving, concise, and user-friendly.
[Structure or Format]: Created a troubleshooting guide with categorized sections and a logical flow of problem-solving steps.

Prompt: As a Documentation Writer, create a troubleshooting guide for a software application. The goal is to assist users in resolving problems and technical difficulties they may encounter. Please provide step-by-step troubleshooting instructions, include relevant error messages, and suggest potential solutions, using a problem-solving, concise, and user-friendly style. Provide a created troubleshooting guide with categorized sections and a logical flow of problem-solving steps.

5.

[Role]: Documentation Writer
[Task]: Draft a developer's guide for integrating a third-party library.
[Context]: The third-party library provides additional functionality for developers' applications.
[Goal]: Help developers understand the library's features, installation process, and integration methods.
[Constraints]: Include code examples, API references, and best practices for using the library.
[Style or Tone]: Technical, informative, and developer-focused.
[Structure or Format]: Drafted a developer's guide with sections on installation, configuration, usage examples, and troubleshooting tips.

Prompt: As a Documentation Writer, draft a developer's guide for integrating a third-party library. The goal is to help developers understand the library's features, installation process, and integration methods. Please include code examples, API references, and best practices for using the library, using a technical, informative, and developer-focused style. Provide a drafted developer's guide with sections on installation, configuration, usage examples, and troubleshooting tips.

6.

[Role]: Documentation Writer
[Task]: Compile a comprehensive FAQ document for a software product.
[Context]: The software product receives frequent inquiries from users.

[Goal]: Provide a centralized resource for addressing common user questions and concerns.
[Constraints]: Cover a wide range of topics, organize the FAQs into categories, and provide clear and concise answers.
[Style or Tone]: Informative, user-friendly, and accessible.
[Structure or Format]: Compiled a comprehensive FAQ document with categorized sections and a searchable index.

Prompt: As a Documentation Writer, compile a comprehensive FAQ document for a software product. The goal is to provide a centralized resource for addressing common user questions and concerns. Please cover a wide range of topics, organize the FAQs into categories, and provide clear and concise answers, using an informative, user-friendly, and accessible style. Provide a compiled comprehensive FAQ document with categorized sections and a searchable index.

7.
[Role]: Documentation Writer
[Task]: Create a user guide for a mobile application.
[Context]: The mobile application has various features and functionalities.
[Goal]: Help users understand and make the most of the application's features.
[Constraints]: Use screenshots, step-by-step instructions, and terminology easily understandable for the target audience.
[Style or Tone]: Clear, concise, and visually engaging.
[Structure or Format]: Created a user guide with chapters, sections, and a visually appealing layout optimized for mobile viewing.

Prompt: As a Documentation Writer, create a user guide for a mobile application. The goal is to help users understand and make the most of the application's features. Please use screenshots, step-by-step instructions, and terminology that is easily understandable for the target audience, using a clear, concise, and visually engaging style. Provide a created user guide with chapters, sections, and a visually appealing layout optimized for mobile viewing.

8.

[Role]: Documentation Writer
[Task]: Develop a troubleshooting manual for a complex hardware system.
[Context]: Assisting users in resolving technical issues efficiently.
[Goal]: Enhance user support and minimize downtime.
[Constraints]: Limited space for troubleshooting steps and technical jargon.
[Style or Tone]: Technical yet accessible, providing clear guidance.
[Structure or Format]: Prepared troubleshooting manual template with logical problem-solving steps.

Prompt: As a Documentation Writer, develop a troubleshooting manual for a complex hardware system. The goal is to enhance user support and minimize downtime. Please consider the limited space for troubleshooting steps and the need for a technical yet accessible style, providing clear guidance. Provide a prepared troubleshooting manual template with logical problem-solving steps.

9.

[Role]: Documentation Writer
[Task]: Develop a style guide for creating consistent technical documentation.
[Context]: The organization produces technical documentation for various products and services.
[Goal]: Ensure consistency in terminology, formatting, and writing style across all technical documentation.
[Constraints]: Cover elements like writing guidelines, document structure, and visual consistency.
[Style or Tone]: Clear, concise, and standardized.
[Structure or Format]: Developed a style guide with rules, examples, and templates for creating consistent technical documentation.

Prompt: As a Documentation Writer, develop a style guide for creating consistent technical documentation. The goal is to ensure consistency in terminology, formatting, and writing style across all technical documentation. Please cover elements like writing guidelines, document structure, and visual consistency, using a clear, concise, and standardized style. Provide a developed style guide with rules, examples, and templates for creating consistent technical documentation.

10.

[Role]: Documentation Writer
[Task]: Write an installation guide for a software application.
[Context]: The software application requires specific steps for installation and configuration.
[Goal]: Assist users in successfully installing and setting up the software application.
[Constraints]: Provide detailed instructions, include system requirements, and troubleshoot common installation issues.
[Style or Tone]: Step-by-step, informative, and user-friendly.
[Structure or Format]: Written an installation guide with sequential steps, screenshots, and troubleshooting tips.

Prompt: As a Documentation Writer, write an installation guide for a software application. The goal is to assist users in successfully installing and setting up the software application. Please provide detailed instructions, include system requirements, and troubleshoot common installation issues, using a step-by-step, informative, and user-friendly style. Provide a written installation guide with sequential steps, screenshots, and troubleshooting tips.

11.

[Role]: Documentation Writer
[Task]: Create a user reference manual for a hardware device.
[Context]: The hardware device has various functions and settings.

[Goal]: Provide users with comprehensive information on how to operate and configure the hardware device.
[Constraints]: Include detailed descriptions, diagrams, and troubleshooting tips.
[Style or Tone]: Informative, user-friendly, and accessible.
[Structure or Format]: Created a user reference manual with chapters, sections, and a visually appealing layout.

Prompt: As a Documentation Writer, create a user reference manual for a hardware device. The goal is to provide users with comprehensive information on how to operate and configure the hardware device. Please include detailed descriptions, diagrams, and troubleshooting tips, using an informative, user-friendly, and accessible style. Provide a created user reference manual with chapters, sections, and a visually appealing layout.

12.
[Role]: Documentation Writer
[Task]: Draft a knowledge base article on frequently asked questions about a web application.
[Context]: The web application receives common inquiries from users.
[Goal]: Provide a self-service resource for users to find answers to their questions.
[Constraints]: Cover a wide range of topics, use clear language, and provide step-by-step instructions where necessary.
[Style or Tone]: Informative, concise, and user-oriented.
[Structure or Format]: Drafted a knowledge base article with categorized sections and a search functionality.

Prompt: As a Documentation Writer, draft a knowledge base article on frequently asked questions about a web application. The goal is to provide a self-service resource for users to find answers to their questions. Please cover a wide range of topics, use clear language, and provide step-by-step instructions where necessary, using an informative, concise, and user-oriented style. Provide a drafted knowledge base article with categorized sections and a search functionality.

13.

[Role]: Documentation Writer
[Task]: Create an onboarding guide for new employees.
[Context]: The onboarding process includes company policies, procedures, and tools.
[Goal]: Help new employees navigate the initial stages of their employment and understand the company's expectations.
[Constraints]: Provide a structured guide, include relevant links and resources, and highlight key information.
[Style or Tone]: Informative, welcoming, and professional.
[Structure or Format]: Created an onboarding guide with sections on company culture, policies, tools, and a checklist.

Prompt: As a Documentation Writer, create an onboarding guide for new employees. The goal is to help new employees navigate the initial stages of their employment and understand the company's expectations. Please provide a structured guide, include relevant links and resources, and highlight key information, using an informative, welcoming, and professional style. Provide a created onboarding guide with sections on company culture, policies, tools, and a checklist.

14.

[Role]: Documentation Writer
[Task]: Write a knowledge base article on troubleshooting common software errors.
[Context]: The software application frequently encounters specific error messages.
[Goal]: Assist users in identifying and resolving common software issues.

[Constraints]: Provide step-by-step troubleshooting instructions, include screenshots, and offer alternative solutions.
[Style or Tone]: Problem-solving, concise, and user-friendly.
[Structure or Format]: Written a knowledge base article with categorized sections and a logical flow of troubleshooting steps.

Prompt: As a Documentation Writer, write a knowledge base article on troubleshooting common software errors. The goal is to assist users in identifying and resolving common software issues. Please provide step-by-step troubleshooting instructions, include screenshots, and offer alternative solutions, using a problem-solving, concise, and user-friendly style. Provide a written knowledge base article with categorized sections and a logical flow of troubleshooting steps.

15.
[Role]: Documentation Writer
[Task]: Develop a template for creating user guides.
[Context]: The organization produces user guides for various products and services.
[Goal]: Establish a consistent and professional format for user guides across the organization.
[Constraints]: Include sections for introduction, features, installation, usage, and troubleshooting.
[Style or Tone]: Clear, structured, and visually appealing.
[Structure or Format]: Developed a user guide template with placeholders for each section and suggested formatting guidelines.

Prompt: As a Documentation Writer, develop a template for creating user guides. The goal is to establish a consistent and professional format for user guides across the organization. Please include sections for introduction, features, installation, usage, and troubleshooting, using a clear, structured, and visually appealing style. Provide a developed user guide template with placeholders for each section and suggested formatting guidelines.

16.

[Role]: Documentation Writer
[Task]: Documenting the New SMS Feature Usage
[Context]: A new SMS feature has been introduced in the product, and users need clear and concise documentation to understand how to use it effectively.
[Goal]: Provide comprehensive instructions and guidelines for users to successfully utilize the new SMS feature and leverage its capabilities.
[Constraints]: Limited space for documentation, varying levels of technical expertise among users.
[Style or Tone]: Clear, user-friendly, and informative.
[Structure or Format]: Step-by-step instructions, screenshots, and code snippets as needed.

Prompt: As a Documentation Writer, your task is to create user-friendly documentation that guides users in effectively using the new SMS feature. Start by introducing the purpose and benefits of the feature, highlighting its potential impact on user experience. Provide step-by-step instructions on how to access and enable the feature, including any necessary configurations or settings. Explain the different functionalities and options available within the feature, such as sending and receiving SMS, managing contacts, and setting up notifications. Accompany the instructions with screenshots and code snippets where relevant to enhance clarity. Anticipate common questions or challenges that users may encounter and address them in troubleshooting or FAQ sections. Your goal is to empower users of varying technical expertise to leverage the new SMS feature efficiently and with confidence.

17.

[Role]: Documentation Writer
[Task]: Write a user manual for a digital product.
[Context]: The digital product has a complex interface and multiple functionalities.

[Goal]: Help users understand and effectively use the digital product.
[Constraints]: Include detailed step-by-step instructions, screenshots, and tips for advanced features.
[Style or Tone]: Clear, comprehensive, and user-oriented.
[Structure or Format]: Written a user manual with chapters, sections, and a visually appealing layout.

Prompt: As a Documentation Writer, write a user manual for a digital product. The goal is to help users understand and effectively use the digital product. Please include detailed step-by-step instructions, screenshots, and tips for advanced features, using a clear, comprehensive, and user-oriented style. Provide a written user manual with chapters, sections, and a visually appealing layout.

18.
[Role]: Documentation Writer
[Task]: Develop a glossary for technical terms used in product documentation.
[Context]: The product documentation contains industry-specific terminology.
[Goal]: Provide a reference resource for users to understand technical terms.
[Constraints]: Define and explain each term concisely, include examples where applicable, and arrange the glossary alphabetically.
[Style or Tone]: Informative, concise, and accessible.
[Structure or Format]: Developed a glossary document with an alphabetized list of technical terms and their definitions.

Prompt: As a Documentation Writer, develop a glossary for technical terms used in product documentation. The goal is to provide a reference resource for users to understand technical terms. Please define and explain each term concisely, include examples where applicable, and arrange the glossary alphabetically, using an informative, concise, and accessible style. Provide a developed glossary document with an alphabetized list of technical terms and their definitions.

19.

[Role]: Documentation Writer
[Task]: Write a troubleshooting guide for common user errors in a software application.
[Context]: Users frequently encounter specific errors while using the software application.
[Goal]: Assist users in identifying and resolving common errors on their own.
[Constraints]: Provide step-by-step troubleshooting instructions, include error code explanations, and offer potential solutions.
[Style or Tone]: Problem-solving, concise, and user-friendly.
[Structure or Format]: Written a troubleshooting guide with categorized sections and a logical flow of troubleshooting steps.

Prompt: As a Documentation Writer, write a troubleshooting guide for common user errors in a software application. The goal is to assist users in identifying and resolving common errors on their own. Please provide step-by-step troubleshooting instructions, include error code explanations, and offer potential solutions, using a problem-solving, concise, and user-friendly style. Provide a written troubleshooting guide with categorized sections and a logical flow of troubleshooting steps.

20.

[Role]: Documentation Writer
[Task]: Create a knowledge base article on best practices for data security.
[Context]: The organization's software product handles sensitive user data.
[Goal]: Educate users on how to protect and maintain the security of their data.
[Constraints]: Cover topics such as password management, encryption, and safe data handling practices.

[Style or Tone]: Informative, authoritative, and actionable.
[Structure or Format]: Created a knowledge base article with sections on different data security topics and practical tips.

Prompt: As a Documentation Writer, create a knowledge base article on best practices for data security. The goal is to educate users on how to protect and maintain the security of their data. Please cover topics such as password management, encryption, and safe data handling practices, using an informative, authoritative, and actionable style. Provide a created knowledge base article with sections on different data security topics and practical tips.

21.
[Role]: Documentation Writer
[Task]: Develop a style guide for consistent writing across all documentation.
[Context]: The organization produces various documentation materials.
[Goal]: Ensure a unified and professional tone in all written documentation.
[Constraints]: Define guidelines for grammar, punctuation, formatting, and voice.
[Style or Tone]: Clear, concise, and consistent.
[Structure or Format]: Developed a style guide document with sections covering grammar rules, formatting guidelines, and tone recommendations.

Prompt: As a Documentation Writer, develop a style guide for consistent writing across all documentation. The goal is to ensure a unified and professional tone in all written documentation. Please define guidelines for grammar, punctuation, formatting, and voice, using a clear, concise, and consistent style. Provide a developed style guide document with sections covering grammar rules, formatting guidelines, and tone recommendations.

22.
[Role]: Documentation Writer
[Task]: Draft a user manual for a hardware device.

[Context]: Guiding users on how to set up and operate the hardware device effectively.
[Goal]: Enhance user understanding and satisfaction with the hardware.
[Constraints]: Limited document length and simplicity in explanations.
[Style or Tone]: Clear, user-friendly, and instructional.
[Structure or Format]: Prepared user manual template with sections for setup and usage instructions.
Prompt: As a Documentation Writer, draft a user manual for a hardware device. The goal is to enhance user understanding and satisfaction with the hardware. Please consider the limited document length and the need for clear, user-friendly, and instructional explanations. Provide a prepared user manual template with sections for setup and usage instructions.

23.
[Role]: Documentation Writer
[Task]: Write a knowledge base article on data backup and recovery procedures.
[Context]: The organization's software product deals with critical user data.
[Goal]: Educate users on how to safeguard and recover their data in case of emergencies.
[Constraints]: Explain backup methods, restoration procedures, and preventive measures.
[Style or Tone]: Informative, practical, and accessible.
[Structure or Format]: Written a knowledge base article with step-by-step instructions and tips for data backup and recovery.

Prompt: As a Documentation Writer, write a knowledge base article on data backup and recovery procedures. The goal is to educate users on how to safeguard and recover their data in case of emergencies. Please explain backup methods, restoration procedures, and preventive measures, using an informative, practical, and accessible style. Provide a written knowledge base article with step-by-step instructions and tips for data backup and recovery.

24.

[Role]: Documentation Writer
[Task]: Create a quick reference guide for keyboard shortcuts in a software application.
[Context]: The software application has several keyboard shortcuts to enhance user productivity.
[Goal]: Provide users with a handy reference for commonly used keyboard shortcuts.
[Constraints]: List the shortcuts with their corresponding functions and organize them logically.
[Style or Tone]: Concise, visually appealing, and easy to navigate.
[Structure or Format]: Created a quick reference guide with a categorized list of keyboard shortcuts and their functions.

Prompt: As a Documentation Writer, create a quick reference guide for keyboard shortcuts in a software application. The goal is to provide users with a handy reference for commonly used keyboard shortcuts. Please list the shortcuts with their corresponding functions and organize them logically, using a concise, visually appealing, and easy-to-navigate style. Provide a created quick reference guide with a categorized list of keyboard shortcuts and their functions.

25.

[Role]: Documentation Writer
[Task]: Draft a user guide for an e-commerce platform.
[Context]: The e-commerce platform allows users to set up online stores and sell products.
[Goal]: Help users understand and navigate the platform's features and functionalities.
[Constraints]: Include sections on store setup, product listing, payment processing, and order management.

[Style or Tone]: User-friendly, step-by-step, and comprehensive.
[Structure or Format]: Drafted a user guide with chapters, subheadings, and screenshots for visual guidance.

Prompt: As a Documentation Writer, draft a user guide for an e-commerce platform. The goal is to help users understand and navigate the platform's features and functionalities. Please include sections on store setup, product listing, payment processing, and order management, using a user-friendly, step-by-step, and comprehensive style. Provide a drafted user guide with chapters, subheadings, and screenshots for visual guidance.

Prompts for Technical Writers

1.

[Role]: Technical Writer
[Task]: Create a software installation guide for a new application.
[Context]: The application requires specific installation steps and system requirements.
[Goal]: Provide users with clear instructions to successfully install the software.
[Constraints]: Include prerequisites, step-by-step installation procedures, and troubleshooting tips.
[Style or Tone]: Detailed, organized, and user-friendly.
[Structure or Format]: Created an installation guide with sections for system requirements, preparation, installation steps, and post-installation checks.

Prompt: As a Technical Writer, create a software installation guide for a new application. The goal is to provide users with clear instructions to successfully install the software. Please include prerequisites, step-by-step installation procedures, and troubleshooting tips, using a detailed, organized, and user-friendly style. Provide a created installation guide with sections for system requirements, preparation, installation steps, and post-installation checks.

2.
[Role]: Technical Writer
[Task]: Write a technical specification document for a new software feature.
[Context]: The software feature involves complex functionalities and interactions.
[Goal]: Provide detailed specifications to guide the development team in implementing the feature.
[Constraints]: Include functional requirements, technical dependencies, and interface specifications.
[Style or Tone]: Precise, concise, and technical.
[Structure or Format]: Written a technical specification document with sections for feature overview, requirements, design, and acceptance criteria.

Prompt: As a Technical Writer, write a technical specification document for a new software feature. The goal is to provide detailed specifications to guide the development team in implementing the feature. Please include functional requirements, technical dependencies, and interface specifications, using a precise, concise, and technical style. Provide a written technical specification document with sections for feature overview, requirements, design, and acceptance criteria.

3.
[Role]: Technical Writer
[Task]: Develop an API documentation for a web service.
[Context]: The web service allows integration with external applications.
[Goal]: Provide developers with comprehensive documentation on how to interact with the API.
[Constraints]: Include endpoints, request/response formats, authentication methods, and error handling.

[Style or Tone]: Technical, informative, and developer-focused.
[Structure or Format]: Developed API documentation with categorized sections, code examples, and API reference.

Prompt: As a Technical Writer, develop an API documentation for a web service. The goal is to provide developers with comprehensive documentation on how to interact with the API. Please include endpoints, request/response formats, authentication methods, and error handling, using a technical, informative, and developer-focused style. Provide a developed API documentation with categorized sections, code examples, and API reference.

4.
[Role]: Technical Writer
[Task]: Write a user guide for a hardware device.
[Context]: The hardware device has various features and configurations.
[Goal]: Help users understand and effectively use the hardware device.
[Constraints]: Provide step-by-step instructions, illustrations, and troubleshooting tips.
[Style or Tone]: Clear, user-friendly, and accessible.
[Structure or Format]: Written a user guide with chapters, sections, and a visually appealing layout.

Prompt: As a Technical Writer, write a user guide for a hardware device. The goal is to help users understand and effectively use the hardware device. Please provide step-by-step instructions, illustrations, and troubleshooting tips, using a clear, user-friendly, and accessible style. Provide a written user guide with chapters, sections, and a visually appealing layout.

5.
[Role]: Technical Writer
[Task]: Create a knowledge base article on common software errors and their solutions.

[Context]: Users frequently encounter specific errors while using the software.
[Goal]: Provide users with troubleshooting guidance to resolve common software errors.
[Constraints]: Explain the causes of each error, provide step-by-step solutions, and include relevant error codes
[Style or Tone]: Informative, concise, and problem-solving.
[Structure or Format]: Created a knowledge base article with sections for different error categories, causes, and solutions.

Prompt: As a Technical Writer, create a knowledge base article on common software errors and their solutions. The goal is to provide users with troubleshooting guidance to resolve common software errors. Please explain the causes of each error, provide step-by-step solutions, and include relevant error codes, using an informative, concise, and problem-solving style. Provide a created knowledge base article with sections for different error categories, causes, and solutions.

6.
[Role]: Technical Writer
[Task]: Write a knowledge base article on designing accessible user interfaces.
[Context]: Assisting UX designers in creating inclusive and accessible designs.
[Goal]: Enhance designers' understanding of accessibility principles and best practices.
[Constraints]: Limited space for comprehensive coverage and simplicity in explanations.
[Style or Tone]: Informative, accessible, and practical.
[Structure or Format]: Prepared knowledge base article template with sections on accessibility guidelines, techniques, and resources.

Prompt: As a Technical Writer, write a knowledge base article on designing accessible user interfaces. The goal is to enhance UX designers' understanding of accessibility principles and best practices. Please consider the limited space for comprehensive coverage and the need for informative, accessible, and practical explanations. Provide a prepared knowledge base article template with sections on accessibility guidelines, techniques, and resources.

7.

[Role]: Technical Writer
[Task]: Write release notes for a software update.
[Context]: The software update introduces new features, improvements, and bug fixes.
[Goal]: Inform users about the changes and enhancements in the software update.
[Constraints]: List new features, improvements, bug fixes, and any known issues or limitations.
[Style or Tone]: Concise, informative, and user-focused.
[Structure or Format]: Written release notes with sections for feature highlights, improvements, bug fixes, and known issues.

Prompt: As a Technical Writer, write release notes for a software update. The goal is to inform users about the changes and enhancements in the software update. Please list new features, improvements, bug fixes, and any known issues or limitations, using a concise, informative, and user-focused style. Provide written release notes with sections for feature highlights, improvements, bug fixes, and known issues.

8.

[Role]: Technical Writer
[Task]: Develop a glossary for a software product.
[Context]: Defining and explaining key terms and concepts.
[Goal]: Enhance user understanding and facilitate product comprehension.

[Constraints]: Limited glossary length and clarity in definitions.
[Style or Tone]: Concise, informative, and easily accessible.
[Structure or Format]: Prepared glossary template with alphabetized terms and concise definitions.

Prompt: As a Technical Writer, develop a glossary for a software product. The goal is to enhance user understanding and facilitate product comprehension. Please consider the limited glossary length and the need for concise, informative, and easily accessible content. Provide a prepared glossary template with alphabetized terms and concise definitions.

9.
[Role]: Technical Writer
[Task]: Develop a troubleshooting guide for a software application.
[Context]: The software application experiences common issues and errors.
[Goal]: Assist users in identifying and resolving software-related problems.
[Constraints]: Provide step-by-step troubleshooting instructions, error code explanations, and common resolutions.
[Style or Tone]: Systematic, problem-solving, and user-friendly.
[Structure or Format]: Developed a troubleshooting guide with categorized sections, FAQs, and step-by-step instructions.

Prompt: As a Technical Writer, develop a troubleshooting guide for a software application. The goal is to assist users in identifying and resolving software-related problems. Please provide step-by-step troubleshooting instructions, error code explanations, and common resolutions, using a systematic, problem-solving, and user-friendly style. Provide a developed troubleshooting guide with categorized sections, FAQs, and step-by-step instructions.

10.
[Role]: Technical Writer
[Task]: Develop a user guide for a prototyping tool.

[Context]: Assisting UX designers in effectively using the prototyping tool to create interactive interfaces.
[Goal]: Improve UX designers' proficiency in prototyping and streamline their workflow.
[Constraints]: Limited document length and clarity in instructions.
[Style or Tone]: User-friendly, step-by-step, and visually enhanced.
[Structure or Format]: Prepared user guide template with sections for tool navigation, features, and best practices.

Prompt: As a Technical Writer, develop a user guide for a prototyping tool. The goal is to improve UX designers' proficiency in prototyping and streamline their workflow. Please consider the limited document length and the need for user-friendly, step-by-step instructions with visual enhancements. Provide a prepared user guide template with sections for tool navigation, features, and best practices.

11.
[Role]: Technical Writer
[Task]: Create a knowledge base article on troubleshooting common network connectivity issues.
[Context]: Users frequently encounter network connectivity problems in their devices.
[Goal]: Provide users with step-by-step troubleshooting instructions to resolve common network connectivity issues.
[Constraints]: Include troubleshooting steps, network configuration settings, and common error messages.
[Style or Tone]: Clear, concise, and technically informative.
[Structure or Format]: Created a knowledge base article with sections for different types of connectivity issues, causes, and troubleshooting steps.

Prompt: As a Technical Writer, create a knowledge base article on troubleshooting common network connectivity issues. The goal is to provide users with step-by-step troubleshooting instructions to resolve common network connectivity issues. Please include troubleshooting steps, network configuration settings, and common error messages, using a clear, concise, and technically informative style. Provide a created knowledge base article with sections for different types of connectivity issues, causes, and troubleshooting steps.

12.

[Role]: Technical Writer
[Task]: Write a user guide for a software development tool.
[Context]: The software development tool helps developers streamline their coding process.
[Goal]: Assist users in understanding and effectively utilizing the software development tool.
[Constraints]: Provide instructions on installation, features, usage examples, and best practices.
[Style or Tone]: Informative, practical, and developer-oriented.
[Structure or Format]: Written a user guide with chapters, sections, code snippets, and visual aids.

Prompt: As a Technical Writer, write a user guide for a software development tool. The goal is to assist users in understanding and effectively utilizing the software development tool. Please provide instructions on installation, features, usage examples, and best practices, using an informative, practical, and developer-oriented style. Provide a written user guide with chapters, sections, code snippets, and visual aids.

13.

[Role]: Technical Writer
[Task]: Develop a troubleshooting FAQ document for a hardware device.
[Context]: The hardware device encounters frequently asked questions and common issues.

[Goal]: Provide users with quick answers and solutions to common hardware device problems.
[Constraints]: Include a list of FAQs, troubleshooting steps, and contact information for support.
[Style or Tone]: Concise, helpful, and user-centric.
[Structure or Format]: Developed a troubleshooting FAQ document with categorized sections and clear answers.

Prompt: As a Technical Writer, develop a troubleshooting FAQ document for a hardware device. The goal is to provide users with quick answers and solutions to common hardware device problems. Please include a list of FAQs, troubleshooting steps, and contact information for support, using a concise, helpful, and user-centric style. Provide a developed troubleshooting FAQ document with categorized sections and clear answers.

14.
[Role]: Technical Writer
[Task]: Write a software user manual for a mobile application.
[Context]: The mobile application has various features and functionalities.
[Goal]: Help users understand and make the most of the mobile application.
[Constraints]: Provide step-by-step instructions, feature descriptions, and screenshots.
[Style or Tone]: User-friendly, informative, and visually appealing.
[Structure or Format]: Written a software user manual with chapters, sections, and illustrations.

Prompt: As a Technical Writer, write a software user manual for a mobile application. The goal is to help users understand and make the most of the mobile application. Please provide step-by-step instructions, feature descriptions, and screenshots, using a user-friendly, informative, and visually appealing style. Provide a written software user manual with chapters, sections, and illustrations.

15.

[Role]: Technical Writer
[Task]: Create a whitepaper on emerging trends in cloud computing.
[Context]: Cloud computing is evolving rapidly with new technologies and practices.
[Goal]: Provide insights into the latest trends and their impact on businesses.
[Constraints]: Include an overview of cloud computing, emerging trends, benefits, and challenges.
[Style or Tone]: Research-based, authoritative, and forward-thinking.
[Structure or Format]: Created a whitepaper with sections for introduction, trends, case studies, and recommendations.

Prompt: As a Technical Writer, create a whitepaper on emerging trends in cloud computing. The goal is to provide insights into the latest trends and their impact on businesses. Please include an overview of cloud computing, emerging trends, benefits, and challenges, using a research-based, authoritative, and forward-thinking style. Provide a created whitepaper with sections for introduction, trends, case studies, and recommendations.

16.

[Role]: Technical Writer
[Task]: Develop a user guide for a software application's API documentation.
[Context]: The software application offers an API for developers to integrate into their projects.
[Goal]: Assist developers in understanding and effectively using the API.
[Constraints]: Include API endpoints, request/response examples, and authentication methods.
[Style or Tone]: Technical, detailed, and developer-friendly.
[Structure or Format]: Developed a user guide with sections for API overview, endpoints, and usage examples.

Prompt: As a Technical Writer, develop a user guide for a software application's API documentation. The goal is to assist developers in understanding and effectively using the API. Please include API endpoints, request/response examples, and authentication methods, using a technical, detailed, and developer-friendly style. Provide a developed user guide with sections for API overview, endpoints, and usage examples.

17.

[Role]: Technical Writer
[Task]: Write a knowledge base article on troubleshooting common software installation issues.
[Context]: Users often encounter difficulties while installing the software application.
[Goal]: Provide users with troubleshooting tips to resolve common software installation issues.
[Constraints]: Include step-by-step troubleshooting instructions, error message explanations, and system requirements.
[Style or Tone]: Informative, step-by-step, and user-focused.
[Structure or Format]: Written a knowledge base article with sections for different installation issues, causes, and solutions.

Prompt: As a Technical Writer, write a knowledge base article on troubleshooting common software installation issues. The goal is to provide users with troubleshooting tips to resolve common software installation issues. Please include step-by-step troubleshooting instructions, error message explanations, and system requirements, using an informative, step-by-step, and user-focused style. Provide a written knowledge base article with sections for different installation issues, causes, and solutions.

18.

[Role]: Technical Writer
[Task]: Create a style guide for a software development team.
[Context]: The style guide aims to ensure consistency and best practices in coding.
[Goal]: Provide guidelines on code formatting, naming conventions, and documentation standards.

[Constraints]: Include examples, explanations, and recommendations for each coding guideline.
[Style or Tone]: Clear, concise, and developer-centric.
[Structure or Format]: Created a style guide with sections for code formatting, naming conventions, and documentation.

Prompt: As a Technical Writer, create a style guide for a software development team. The goal is to provide guidelines on code formatting, naming conventions, and documentation standards. Please include examples, explanations, and recommendations for each coding guideline, using a clear, concise, and developer-centric style. Provide a created style guide with sections for code formatting, naming conventions, and documentation.

19.
[Role]: Technical Writer
[Task]: Write a user guide for a project management software.
[Context]: The project management software helps teams collaborate and manage tasks.
[Goal]: Assist users in effectively utilizing the project management software.
[Constraints]: Provide instructions on project setup, task management, and collaboration features.
[Style or Tone]: Informative, organized, and user-friendly.
[Structure or Format]: Written a user guide with chapters, sections, and visual aids.

Prompt: As a Technical Writer, write a user guide for a project management software. The goal is to assist users in effectively utilizing the project management software. Please provide instructions on project setup, task management, and collaboration features, using an informative, organized, and user-friendly style. Provide a written user guide with chapters, sections, and visual aids.

20.

[Role]: Technical Writer
[Task]: Develop a release notes document for a software update.
[Context]: The software update introduces new features, bug fixes, and improvements.
[Goal]: Inform users about the changes and enhancements in the software update.
[Constraints]: Include a list of new features, resolved issues, and known limitations.
[Style or Tone]: Clear, concise, and user-oriented.
[Structure or Format]: Created a release notes document with sections for feature highlights, bug fixes, and known issues.

Prompt: As a Technical Writer, develop a release notes document for a software update. The goal is to inform users about the changes and enhancements in the software update. Please include a list of new features, resolved issues, and known limitations, using a clear, concise, and user-oriented style. Provide a created release notes document with sections for feature highlights, bug fixes, and known issues.

21.

[Role]: Technical Writer
[Task]: Create a developer's guide for integrating an API into a web application.
[Context]: Developers need guidance on how to use the API in their web projects.
[Goal]: Assist developers in understanding the API's functionalities and implementing it effectively.
[Constraints]: Include API documentation, authentication methods, request/response examples, and error handling.
[Style or Tone]: Developer-friendly, informative, and practical.
[Structure or Format]: Created a developer's guide with sections for API overview, integration steps, and code samples.

Prompt: As a Technical Writer, create a developer's guide for integrating an API into a web application. The goal is to assist developers in understanding the API's functionalities and implementing it effectively. Please include API documentation, authentication methods, request/response examples, and error handling, using a developer-friendly, informative, and practical style. Provide a created developer's guide with sections for API overview, integration steps, and code samples.

22.

[Role]: Technical Writer
[Task]: Write a software troubleshooting guide for common error messages.
[Context]: Users frequently encounter specific error messages while using the software.
[Goal]: Provide users with step-by-step instructions to resolve common software errors.
[Constraints]: Include error message explanations, possible causes, and troubleshooting steps.
[Style or Tone]: Clear, concise, and user-focused.
[Structure or Format]: Written a troubleshooting guide with sections for different error messages and corresponding solutions.

Prompt: As a Technical Writer, write a software troubleshooting guide for common error messages. The goal is to provide users with step-by-step instructions to resolve common software errors. Please include error message explanations, possible causes, and troubleshooting steps, using a clear, concise, and user-focused style. Provide a written troubleshooting guide with sections for different error messages and corresponding solutions.

23.

[Role]: Technical Writer
[Task]: Write a step-by-step user guide for a software feature.

[Context]: Assisting users in utilizing a specific functionality.
[Goal]: Enable users to effectively utilize the feature for their needs.
[Constraints]: Limited guide length and simplicity in instructions.
[Style or Tone]: Clear, concise, and action-oriented.
[Structure or Format]: Prepared user guide template with sections for feature overview, setup, and step-by-step instructions.

Prompt: As a Technical Writer, write a step-by-step user guide for a software feature. The goal is to enable users to effectively utilize the feature for their needs. Please consider the limited guide length and the need for clear, concise, and action-oriented content. Provide a prepared user guide template with sections for feature overview, setup, and step-by-step instructions.

24.
[Role]: Technical Writer
[Task]: Write a knowledge base article on optimizing website performance.
[Context]: Website owners seek to improve their website's speed and overall performance.
[Goal]: Provide website owners with practical tips to optimize their website's performance.
[Constraints]: Include caching techniques, image optimization, code minification, and server configuration.
[Style or Tone]: Informative, actionable, and webmaster-oriented.
[Structure or Format]: Written a knowledge base article with sections for different performance optimization techniques.

Prompt: As a Technical Writer, write a knowledge base article on optimizing website performance. The goal is to provide website owners with practical tips to optimize their website's performance. Please include caching techniques, image optimization, code minification, and server configuration, using an informative, actionable, and webmaster-oriented style. Provide a written knowledge base article with sections for different performance optimization techniques.

25.

[Role]: Technical Writer

[Task]: Create a system administrator's guide for a network security software.

[Context]: System administrators need detailed instructions on deploying and managing the security software.

[Goal]: Assist system administrators in effectively setting up and maintaining the network security software.

[Constraints]: Include installation instructions, configuration options, security policies, and troubleshooting tips.

[Style or Tone]: Technical, comprehensive, and administrator-focused.

[Structure or Format]: Created a system administrator's guide with chapters, sections, and configuration examples.

Prompt: As a Technical Writer, create a system administrator's guide for a network security software. The goal is to assist system administrators in effectively setting up and maintaining the network security software. Please include installation instructions, configuration options, security policies, and troubleshooting tips, using a technical, comprehensive, and administrator-focused style. Provide a created system administrator's guide with chapters, sections, and configuration examples.

Chapter 7: Continuing the Journey

As we conclude this playbook, it is important to acknowledge that the field of AI (and UX design) is ever-evolving. New advancements and research in the field continue to push the boundaries of what's possible. Staying up-to-date with the latest developments and exploring emerging resources will be crucial to mastering the art of AI-powered UX design.

Fortunately, there are numerous resources available to help you continue your journey. Online communities, forums, books, blogs, articles, courses, YouTube tutorials, GitHub, and AI-related conferences provide platforms for knowledge sharing and learning that will serve to deepen your understanding of generative AI and the science of prompt engineering. Additionally, OpenAI's documentation and research papers offer invaluable insights into the workings of language models such as ChatGPT.

Looking ahead, the future of AI holds immense potential. Researchers are constantly striving to refine and enhance language models, exploring new approaches to improve natural language understanding and generating more contextually relevant responses. With ongoing developments in AI ethics, transparency, and explainability, the responsible and ethical use of AI will remain at the forefront of the AI community's endeavors.

In closing, "The ChatGPT Playbook: Mastering Prompts for Exceptional UX Design" serves as a stepping stone in your journey toward mastering AI-powered UX design. Armed with the knowledge and techniques shared in this book, you are well-equipped to create exceptional user experiences that seamlessly blend human *and* artificial intelligence. Embrace the ever-evolving landscape of AI, stay curious, and continue to push the boundaries of what's possible in the realm of UX design.

About the Author

Lorraine Phillips is a multi-disciplined UX professional with over a decade's worth of experience working with and consulting for digital agencies, startups, small businesses, and Fortune 500 companies. With an MBA in business administration, a BS in computer science, and an AA in graphic design, Lorraine brings a diverse range of skills and expertise to her work.

As an author Lorraine has received several awards where her books have been recognized for exhibiting superior levels of creativity and originality as well as high standards of design and production quality. She was previously selected for one of the country's most respected book awards, being named an IBPA Benjamin Franklin Awards silver finalist in the Business and Economics category for excellence in book editorial and design

As a dynamic speaker, author, freelancer, and coach, it is Lorraine's mission to help others achieve their personal and professional dreams. As she puts it in her own words, "It's exactly what I was born to do!"

Index

A

B

C

D

E

F

L

M

N

O

R

S

T

U

V

W

Y

www.ingramcontent.com/pod-product-compliance
Ingram Content Group UK Ltd.
Pitfield, Milton Keynes, MK11 3LW, UK
UKHW062259290726
14090UKWH00017B/782